COUNTY RED BOOK

WORCESTERSHIRE

TOWN CENTRE MAPS

Street maps with index
Administrative Districts
Road Map with index
Postcodes

Red Books showing the way

Every effort has been made to verify the accuracy of information in this book but the publishers cannot accept responsibility for expense or loss caused by an error or omission.

Information that will be of assistance to the user of the maps will be welcomed.

The representation on these maps of a road, track or path is no evidence of the existence of a right of way.

Street plans prepared and published by ESTATE PUBLICATIONS, Bridewell House, TENTERDEN, KENT. The Publishers acknowledge the co-operation of the local authorities of towns represented in this atlas.

Ordnance Survey® This product includes mapping data licensed from Ordnance Survey® with the permission of the Controller of Her Majesty's Stationery Office.

www.ESTATE-PUBLICATIONS.co.uk

Printed by Ajanta Offset, New Delhi, India.

LEGEND

	...thanized / Restricted Access
	Track
	Built Up Area
- - - - -	Footpath
	Stream
	River
Lock	Canal
	Railway / Station
●	Post Office
P P+	Car Park / Park & Ride
C	Public Convenience
+	Place of Worship
→	One-way Street
i	Tourist Information Centre
8 8	Adjoining Pages
	Area Depicting Enlarged Centre
	Emergency Services
	Industrial Buildings
	Leisure Buildings
	Education Buildings
	Hotels etc.
	Retail Buildings
	General Buildings
	Woodland
	Orchard
	Recreation Ground
	Cemetery

C000312098

COUNTY RED BOOKS contain street maps for each town centre. The street atlases listed below are SUPER & LOCAL RED BOOKS, with comprehensive local coverage.

KIDDERMINSTER

including: Bewdley, Blakedown, Hartlebury, Stourport-on-Severn etc.

REDDITCH & BROMSGROVE

including: Astwood Bank, Barnt Green, Callow Hill, Church Hill, Studley, Wychbold etc.

WEST MIDLANDS / BIRMINGHAM

including: Bedworth, Birmingham, Bromsgrove, Cannock, Coventry, Dudley, Hinckley, Kenilworth, Kidderminster, Lichfield, Nuneaton, Redditch, Royal Leamington Spa, Solihull, Tamworth, Walsall, Warwick, Wolverhampton etc.

WORCESTER

including: Droitwich, Fernhill Heath, Great Malvern, Kempsey, Lower Broadheath etc.

For a complete title listing please visit our website
www.estate-publications.co.uk

CONTENTS 3

Scale of street plans: 4 Inches to 1 Mile (unless otherwise stated)

COUNTY RED BOOKS

This atlas is intended for those requiring street maps of the historical and commercial centres of towns within the county. Each locality is normally presented on one or two pages and although, with many small towns, this space is sufficient to portray the whole urban area, the maps of large towns and cities are for centres only and are not intended to be comprehensive. Such coverage is offered in the Super and Local Red Book (see Page 2).

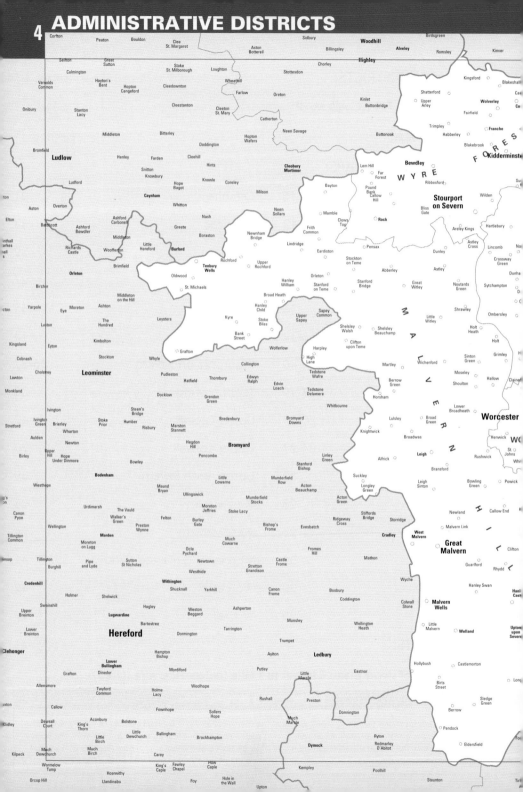

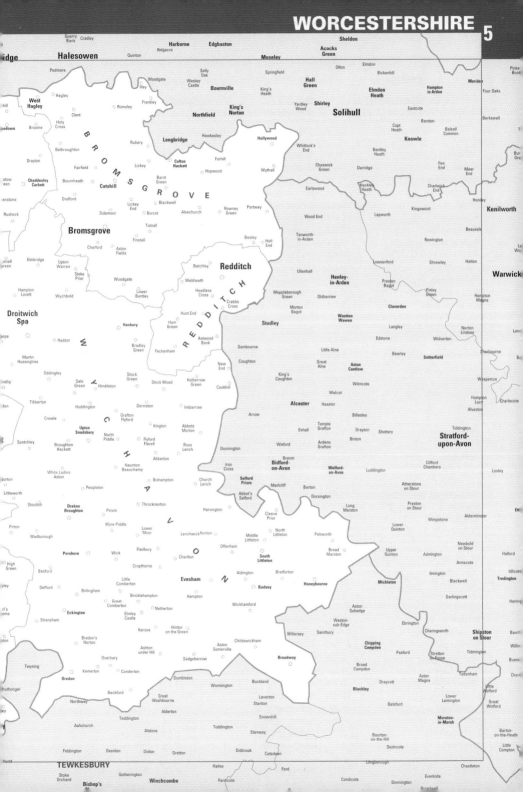

County of Worcestershire, estimated population **542,107**

Districts: Boundaries of the districts are shown on pages 4-5.

Bromsgrove	**87,837**	Worcester	**93,353**
Malvern Hills	**72,172**	Wychavon	**112,957**
Redditch	**78,807**	Wyre Forest	**96,981**

Population figures are based upon 2001 Census.

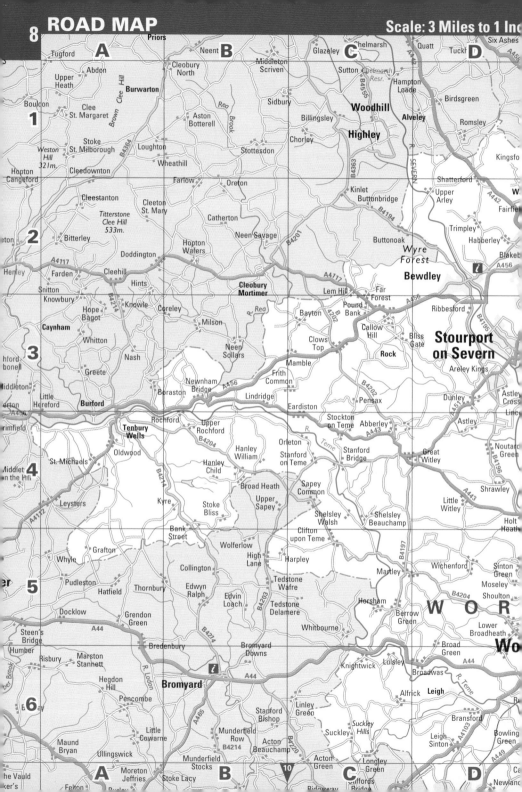

A   **B**   **C**   **D**

Priors

Tugford   Neent   Glazeley   Chelmarsh   Quatt   Tuckf   Six Ashes

Cleobury North   Middleton Scriven   Sutton   Chelmarsh Resr.   Hampton Loade

Abdon   Burwarton

Upper Heath   Sidbury   Woodhill   Alveley   Birdsgreen

Clee St. Margaret   Aston Botterell   Billingsley   Highley   Upper Arley   Romsley

1

Boulcon   Rea Brook   Chorley   Kingsfo

Hopton Cangeford   Weston Hill 321m.   Stoke St. Milborough   Loughton   Stottesdon   Kinlet   Shatterford

Cleedownton   Wheathill   Oreton   Buttonbridge   Upper Arley   Fairfiel

Farlow   Cleestanton   Cleeton St. Mary   Catherton   Neen Savage   Buttonoak   Trimpley   Habberley

2

Bitterley   Titterstone Clee Hill 533m.   Hopton Wafers   Wyre Forest   Blakel

Henley   Doddington   Cleobury Mortimer   Bewdley

Farden   Cleehill   Hints   Lem Hill   Far Forest

Snitton   Knowbury   Knowle   Coreley   Milson   Bayton   Pound Bank   Ribbesford

Hope Bagot   Clows Top   Callow Hill   Bliss Gate   Stourport on Severn

Caynham   Whitton   Nash   Neen Sollars   Mamble   Rock   Areley Kings

3

Greete   Frith Common   Dunley   Astley Cross

Middleton   Little Hereford   Newnham Bridge   Lindridge   Eardiston   Pensax   Astley   Line

Burford   Boraston   Stockton on Teme   Abberley

Rochford   Upper Rochford   Orleton   Stanford Bridge   Great Witley   Noutar Green

Tenbury Wells   Hanley William   Stanford on Teme

4

St. Michaels   Oldwood   Hanley Child   Broad Heath   Sapey Common   Little Witley   Shrawley

Leysters   Kyre   Stoke Bliss   Upper Sapey   Shelsley Walsh   Shelsley Beauchamp   Holt Heath

Bank Street   Wolferlow   Clifton upon Teme

Whyle   Grafton   High Lane   Harpley   Martley   Wichenford   Sinton Green

5

Pudleston   Collington   Tedstone Wafre   Moseley   Shoulton

Hatfield   Thornbury   Edwyn Ralph   Edvin Loach   Tedstone Delamere   Horsham   Berrow Green   W O R

Docklow   Grendon Green   Whitbourne   Broad Green   Lower Broadheath

Steen's Bridge   Bredenbury   Bromyard Downs   Knightwick   Lulsley   Broadwas   Wo

Humber   Risbury   Marston Stannett   Alfrick   Leigh

Hegdon Hill   Bromyard   Linley Green

6

Maund Bryan   Pencombe   Little Cowarne   Stanford Bishop   Suckley Hills   Bransford

Ullingswick   Munderfield Row   Acton Beauchamp   Suckley   Leigh Sinton   Bowling Green

Vauld   Moreton Jeffries   Stoke Lacy   Munderfield Stocks   Acton Green   Longley Green   A449

Felton   Ridgeway   Cliffords Bridge   Newlan

A   **B**   **10**   **C**   **D**

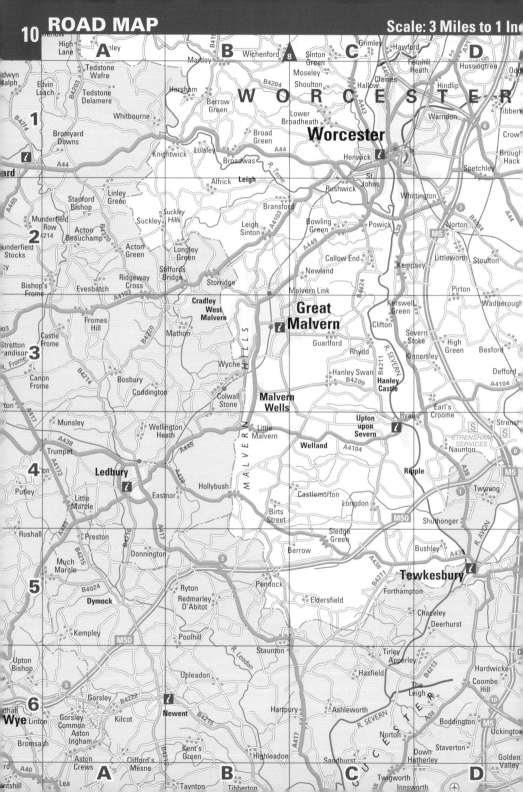

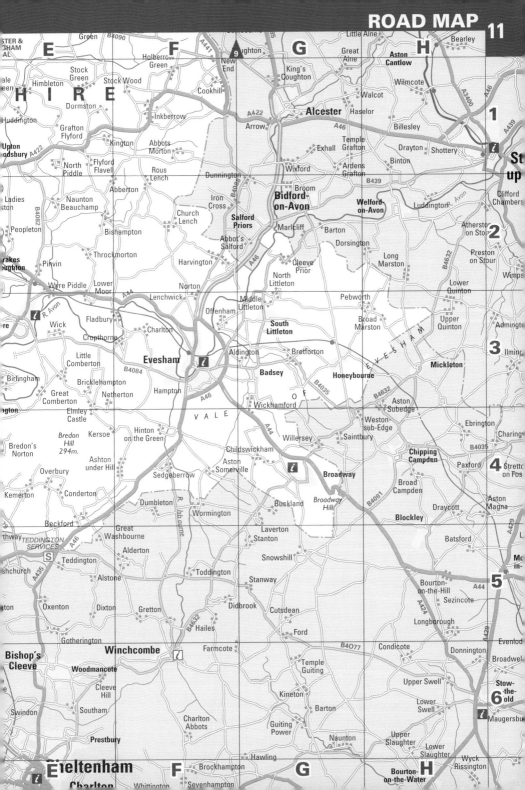

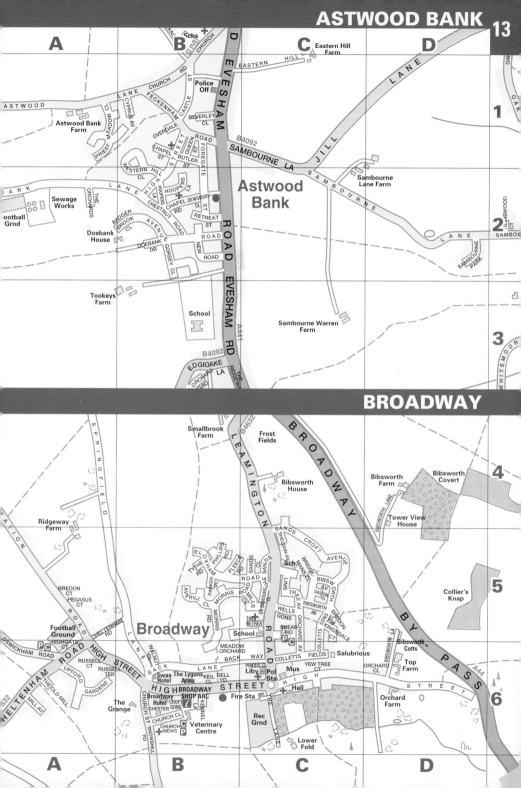

BROADWAY

Astwood Bank (top map)

A
B
Schs
Church
C Eastern Hill Farm
D

ASTWOOD
Church Lane
Feckenham
Castle St
Police Off
Eastern Hill
Beverley Cl
B4092
Sambourne La
Jill Lane
Oak

Astwood Bank Farm
Priest Meadow Cl
Cyprus Av
Overdale
Chapel St
Street
Queen St
Butler
Foregate
Road
Sambourne Lane Farm

Western Hill
High St
Hoopers La
Chapel Dewsbury St
Astwood Bank
Sambourne Lane
Astwood Cl
Samboi

The Orchards
Badger Brook Cl
Chestnut Road
Retreat St
Road
Lane
Sambourne Park

Sewage Works
Avenue
Gorsey Cl
Doebank Dr
New Road

Football Grnd
Doebank House

Tookeys Farm
School
Evesham Rd
B4092
A441
Sambourne Warren Farm
Whitemoor

EDGIOAKE
Orchard La
The Ridgeway

Broadway (bottom map)

A
B
C
D

Spring Field
Smallbrook Farm
Leamington
B4632
Frost Fields
BROADWAY
Bibsworth Farm
Bibsworth Covert

Ridgeway Farm
Bibsworth House
Bibsworth Lane
Tower View House
Collier's Knap

Bredon Ct
Pegasus Ct
Bloxham Rd
Tythe Rd
Phillips
Parker Cl
Averill Cl
Morris
Fleece Rd
Road
Sands
Sands
Saviours Cl
Croft Avenue
Sheldon Av
Mains Cl
Bridge
Bibsworth Av
Daston Cl
Lime
Tree Av
Bibsworth Av
Brendon Cl
Kingsdale Ct

Football Ground
Highgate Ct
Cheltenham Rd
Road
High Street
Broadway
Wells Gdns
The Retreat
School
Shear Rd
Colletts Gdns
Orchard Av
Salubrious
Bibsworth Cotts
Top Farm
By-Pass
A44

Dswickham Road
Lifford Gardens
Russell Ter
Russell Ct
Chester St
Walnut Lane
Back Lane
Meadow Orchard
Way
Colletts Fields
Yew Tree
Orchard Cl
Orchard Farm
Street

Cheltenham Road
The Old Mill
Mill Av
The Grange
Swan Hotel
The Lygons Arms
Broadway Hotel
Chester Gdns
Keil Croft
Bell Cl
Shop Arc
Kennel Lane
Church Cl
Church Mews
Snowshill Rd
Veterinary Centre
High Street
Liby
Pol Sta
Mus
Hall
Fire Sta
Rec Grnd
Lower Fold

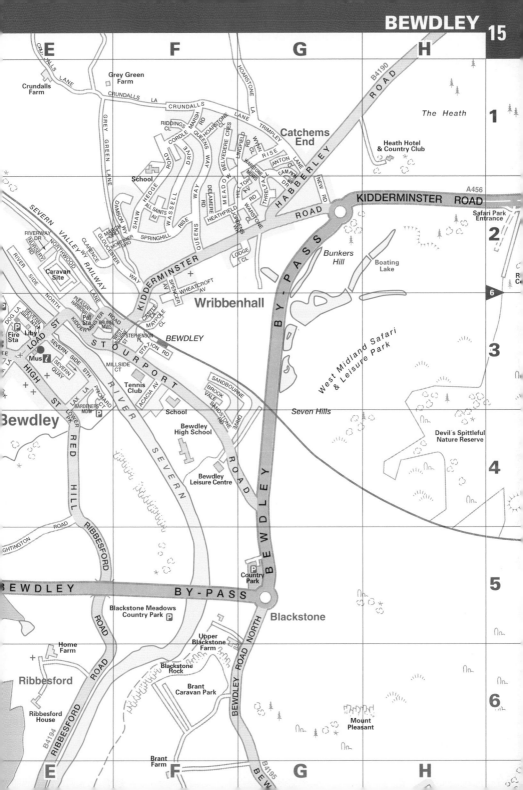

E **F** **G** **H**

1

Crundalls Farm

Grey Green Farm

CRUNDALLS LANE

CRUNDALLS LA

CRUNDALLS LA

HOARSTONE LANE

B4190 ROAD

The Heath

RIDDINGS CL

CORDLE MARSH RD

HOARSTONE

TRIMPLEY RISE

Catchems End

Heath Hotel & Country Club

School

QUEENS WAY

DANSON WY

SHAW HEDGE ROAD

BELVEDERE CRES

ENGFIELD

WYNN RD

WARSTONE

HILLTOP AV

THRELFALL

ANTON CL

CAMP RV

HABBERLEY

NEW RD

LANE

ROAD

A456

2

SEVERN VALLEY RAILWAY

RIVERWAY

NORTHWOOD DR

RIVER SIDE RD

Caravan Site

GREY GREEN LANE

MARSH RD

CLARENCE

GLOUCESTER

KITCHENER GRO

SPRINGHILL

MEADOW

HEATHFIELD

DELAMERE RD

WASSELL RD

RISE

QUEENS WAY

LODGE CL

LODGE CL

WHEATCROFT AV

SPENCER AV

KIDDERMINSTER

ROAD

BY-PASS

ROAD

KIDDERMINSTER ROAD

Safari Park Entrance

Bunkers Hill

Boating Lake

6

R C

3

DOG LA

Fire Sta

Liby

LOAD ST

HIGH ST

SEVERN SIDE NTH

PLEASANT HARBOUR

KIDDERMINSTER MWS

STOURPORT ROAD

Pol Sta

BRUNEL CL

STEPHENSON CT

CASTLE

MAPOLE CL

STATION RD

BEWDLEY

Wribbenhall

Mus i

SEVERN QUAY

MILLSIDE CT

Tennis Club

ACACIA AV

SANDBOURNE

BROOK VALE

SANDSTONE

DRIVE

West Midland Safari & Leisure Park

Seven Hills

Devil's Spittleful Nature Reserve

4

Bewdley

LOWER PK RD

RED HILL

ORCHARD

GARDENERS MDW

School

Bewdley High School

Bewdley Leisure Centre

RIBBESFORD

ROAD

SEVERN

BEWDLEY ROAD

5

BEWDLEY BY-PASS

GHTINGTON ROAD

Blackstone Meadows Country Park

Country Park

Blackstone

RIBBESFORD ROAD

Home Farm

Ribbesford

Upper Blackstone Farm

Blackstone Rock

Brant Caravan Park

BEWDLEY ROAD NORTH

Mount Pleasant

6

B4194 RIBBESFORD ROAD

Ribbesford House

Brant Farm

B4195 BEW

E **F** **G** **H**

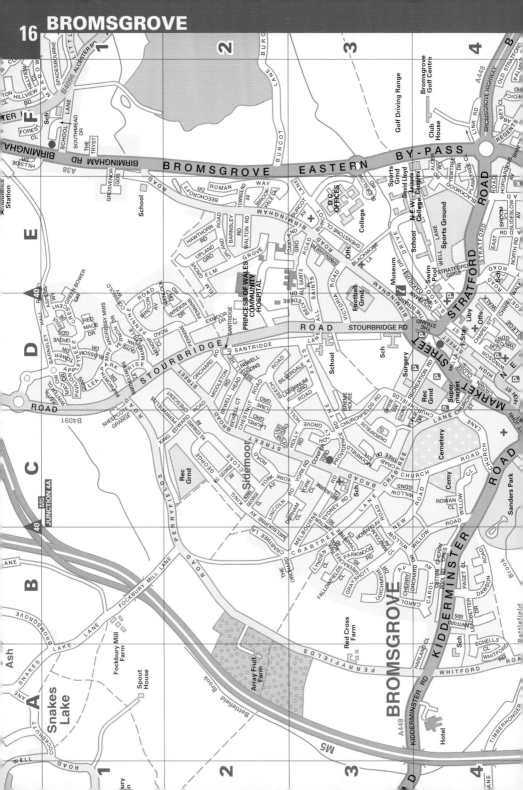

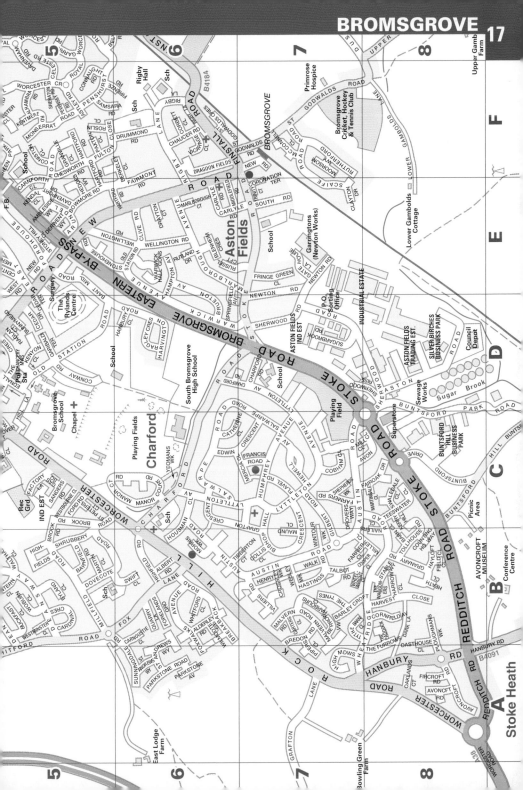

Lenchwick Cottage

Lenchwick

Shepherd's Plantation

Black Monk Lakes

THE PADDOCKS

KINGS LA

KINGS

Football Field

Club

St Egwins

HEATHFIELD

LLOYD

ROAD B4088

A461

ROAD

Whiteladies

Lenchwick House

EVESHAM

Evesham Country Park

Helip

Twyford

Manor Farm

The Mill House

A44

Chadbury Lock

THE

Leicester Tower

Abbey Manor House

Obelisk

Battle of Evesham 1265

SQUIRES

GREENHILL

EVESHAM

BLAYNEYS LANE

ABBOTSWOOD

SIMON DE MONTFORT DR

Oxstalls Cottage

WORCESTER

River Avon

Abbey Manor Farm

Rawlings Farm

Greenhill

GREENHILL

PARK ROAD

GREENHILL TER

COLLINSFIELD

PRINCE HENRY CL

PRINCE EDWARDS CL

Hampton Parks Farm

Works

School

LANESFIELD PK

LANESFIELD ROAD

CROFT

Sewage Works

Depot

ST CHRISTOPHER COURT

School

ROAD

WORCE

BRI

A4184

GREENHILL

THE GARDENS

WINDSOR RD

BALMORAL CL

SANDRINGHAM CL

VICTORIA

PRINCESS

WDSOR RD

22

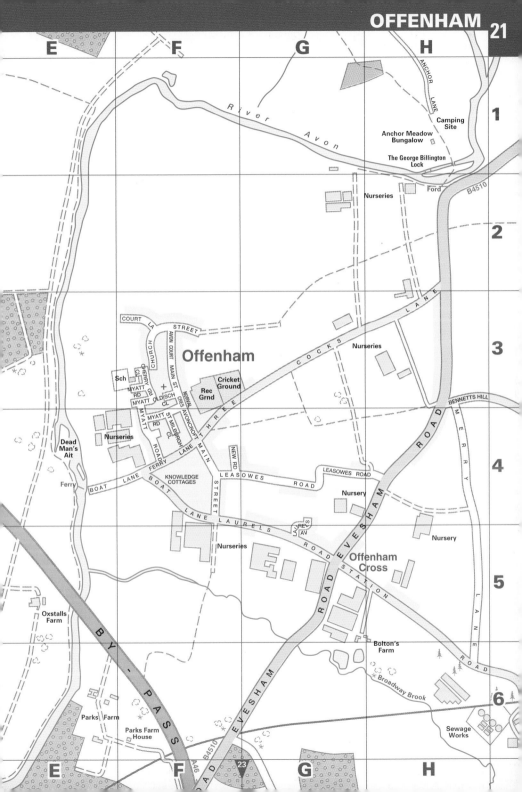

E   F   G   H

1

2

3

4

5

6

River Avon

ANCHOR LANE

Camping Site

Anchor Meadow Bungalow

The George Billington Lock

Ford

B4510

Nurseries

COURT LA

STREET

AVON COURT

CHURCH

Offenham

COCKS LANE

Nurseries

Sch

MYATT RD

CHERRY RD

MAIN ST

OLD SCH CL

NORVAL CRES

ST MILBURGH CL

AVONCROFT

Cricket Ground

Rec Grnd

THREE

BENNETTS HILL

ROAD

MERRY

MYATT RD

MYATT RD

Nurseries

Dead Man's Ait

FERRY LANE

MAIN

STREET

NEW RD

LEASOWES

ROAD

LEASOWES ROAD

Nursery

Ferry

BOAT LANE

BOAT

KNOWLEDGE COTTAGES

Nursery

LANE

LAURELS

ROAD

LAURELS AV

STATION

EVESHAM

Offenham Cross

Nurseries

Oxstalls Farm

BY - PASS

ROAD

Bolton's Farm

LANE

ROAD

Broadway Brook

Sewage Works

Parks Farm

EVESHAM

Parks Farm House

B4510

A46

ROAD

23

E   F   G   H

EVESHAM

Hampton

Fairfield

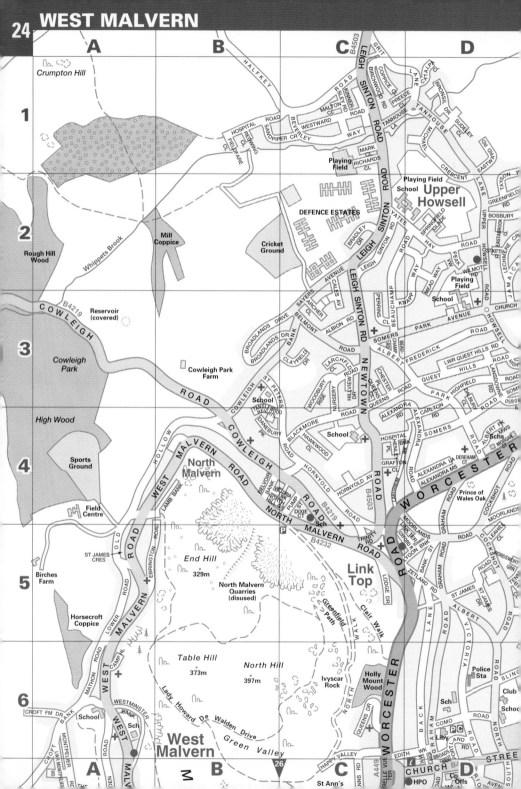

A   **B**   **C**   **D**

1

Crumpton Hill

HALFKEY

HOSPITAL

FIELDFARE

REDWING

SANDPIPER

BEVERLEY

MALTON

WESTWARD

KINNERSLEY RD

CRESLEY

ROAD

BIRCHWOOD RD

COPPICE RD

PREECE CL

LEIGH

SINTON

GRIT

CALPA

CATALPA

TANHOUSE LA

MICHAEL

BRONSIL DR

SUDELEY CL

EASTWAY

CRESCENT

Playing Field

MARK
RICHARDS CL

Playing Field

School

Upper Howsell

TAYSON RD

GREENFIELD

BOSBURY

UPPER

CHURCH

2

Rough Hill Wood

Whippets Brook

Mill Coppice

Cricket Ground

DEFENCE ESTATES

YATES

BRADLEY DR

LEIGH

SINTON

SINTON RD

LEIGH

AVENUE

CALES AV

HAY

WAY

MEAD WAY

PEAK

PERRINS

KNAPP

BEAUCHAMP

SOMERS

PARK AVENUE

WILMOTL

Playing Field

School

HOWSELL RD

JAMAICA

LECHMERE

KITTSERE

3

B4219

COWLEIGH

Reservoir (covered)

Cowleigh Park

Cowleigh Park Farm

BROADLANDS DRIVE

BROADLANDS

SAYERS

ARCHER

BELMONT

ALBION

CLAYFIELD

BANK

ROAD

ST PETERS

School

TANGLEWOOD HEIGHTS

DANEBURY PK

WOODBURY

HILLVIEW RD

RISE

NURSERY

LARCHFIELD

CL

CHESTER RD

NEWTOWN

QUEENS

ALBERT

FREDERICK

LWR QUEST HILLS RD

QUEST HILLS

PARK HIGHFIELD

LANSDOWNE RD

DALBURY

ROAD

SOM

OSBO

4

High Wood

Sports Ground

Field Centre

HOLLOW

WEST

MALVERN

ROAD

COWLEIGH

ROAD

LAMB BANK

North Malvern

BELVOIR

BANK

VICTORIA

HILLS

PUMP ST

DIXIE

ST

BLACKMORE

HAWKWOOD CL

HORNYOLD

School

HENLEY

HOSPITAL PL

GRAFTON

HORNYOLD AV

ROAD

B4503

CARLTON RD

ALEXANDRA

SOMERS

ALEXANDRA MS

ALEXANDRA LA

DEREHAM

CL

ALBERT PK

Schs

MORGAN

MWS

CT

WORCESTER

Prince of Wales Oak

COCKSHOT

MOORLANDS

5

Birches Farm

ST JAMES CRES

OLD

ROAD

EBRINGTON

LOWER

MALVERN

ROAD

Horsecroft Coppice

End Hill
329m

North Malvern Quarries (disused)

NORTH

MALVERN

ROAD

B4219

B4232

TRINITY RD

LODGE DR

Greenfield Path

Link Top

CLAIT

WALK

WALK

MOORLANDS

OXFORD RD

LINK TER

BANK

ZETLAND RD

GRAHAM ROAD

GRAHAM RD

ST JAMES DR

ALBERT

VICTORIA

ROAD

COCKSHOT

CL

LEAMLE

WORDSWORTH

GRN

6

CROFT FM BANK

MONTPELIER

LWR MONTPELIER

MATHON

ROAD

CAMP HL

WEST

WESTMINSTER

BANK

School

Sch

WEST MALVERN

Table Hill
373m

Lady Howard De Walden Drive

North Hill
397m

Ivyscar Rock

Green Valley

HAPPY VALLEY

St Ann's

QUEENS DR

Holly Mount Wood

NORTH

WORCESTER

ROAD

BACK

GRAHAM

EDITH WK

BELLE VUE

A449

HPO

CHURCH STREE

Co Offs

PC

Liby

Police Sta

Club

School

VICTORIA

COMO RD

ROAD

Sch

SLING

NORTH

AVEN

E   F   G   Cricket Ground   H

Elms Farm

Lower Howsell

Newland

Beauchamp Almshouses

Madresfield Brook

Sports Ground

School

Cricket Ground

Superstores

Madford Retail Park

Madresfield

University Wood

Malvern Link

Spring Lane Industrial Estate

Victoria Park

Factory

Playing Field

Kettlepin Rough

Link Common

MALVERN LINK

Fire Sta

Schools   Playing Field

Cricket Ground

North End

Walmer Wood

GREAT MALVERN

Football Ground

Sherrard's Green

Moat Pond

Playing Field

Moat   Moat Court

MADRESFIELD ROAD

Playing Field

Cemetery

27 Dyves Meadow Air Training

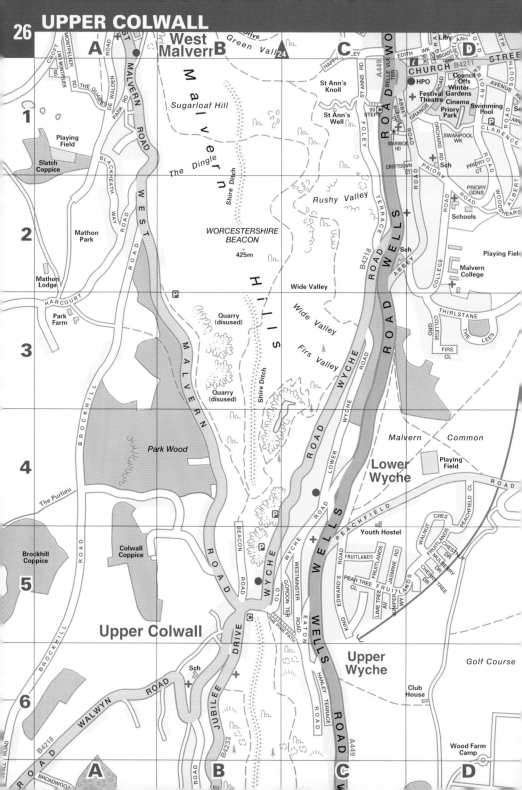

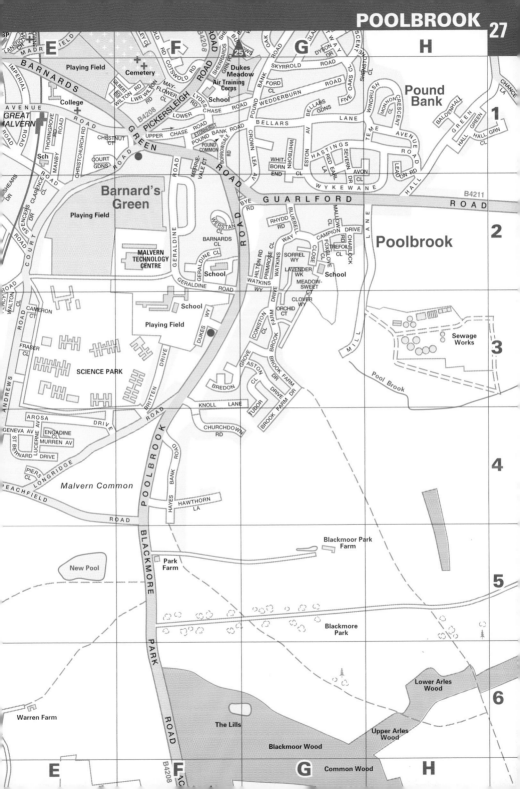

This page is a street map of the Hollywood / Wythall area.

Grid references: A B C D across the top and bottom; 1 2 3 4 5 6 down the right side.

Major labelled areas and features:
- Golf Course
- Club House
- Hollywood
- Truemans Heath Farm
- Truemans Heath
- Little Truemans Heath Farm
- Bateman's Green
- Ridge Farm
- Ashmount Farm
- Bateman's Green Farm
- Holly Tree Farm
- Wood Leaves Farm
- Firtree Farm
- Drake's Cross
- Schools
- Playing Field
- Wythall Park
- Holly Farm
- Silver Street
- Depot
- Drakes Cross Parade
- Wythall House
- Barn Hill House
- Grimes Hill
- Bleakhouse Farm
- Manor Farm
- Wythall
- Birmingham & Midland Museum of Transport
- Britannic Assurance
- Cemy
- Football Ground
- Heath Farm
- Lowbridge
- Norton

Road names include: Alcester Road, Hollywood By-Pass, Slough Lane, Dark Lane, Love Lane, Packhorse Lane, Baccabox Lane, New Orchard Way, Alfreda Av, Woodleaves, Hollywood Lane, Links Road, Simon Road, Kenway, Dyas Road, Fenton Road, Easton Gro, Lynbrook Cl, Windrush Road, Cropthorne Dr, Richmond Rd, Berrymound Vw, Mayhurst Rd, Wythwood Rd, Houndsfield Lane, Truemans Heath Lane, Shawhurst Lane, Corbett Road, Mill Cl, Chantry Cl, Fieldways, May Farm Cl, Laburnum Trees, Oak Trees, May Trees, Poplar Trees, Elmwood, Beaudesert, The Hurst, Arden Rd, Warming-ton Rd, Shawhurst Cft, Forest, Hawthorne, Wood Croft, Beech Drive, Silver Birch, Alder Cl, Oak Tree La, Sycamore Drive, Hazel, Bramley Dr, Cherry Wk, Aspen Gro, Hadley Cl, Houndsfield Ct, Labur-num Cl, Rowan Cl, The Reddings, Shawfield, The Myners, Rye Cl, Falstaff Rd, Burford Rd, Paddocks, Oakwood, The Willows, Sims Rd, Kiln Lane, Wilmore Lane, Brick Lane, Gorsey Lane, Manor Rd, Meadow Ann, Church Cl, Chapel Dr, Station Road, Three Oaks Rd, Lea Green Lane, Littleshaw La, The Spinney, Selsdon Cl, Green Lane, Silver Street, Batemans Lane, A435

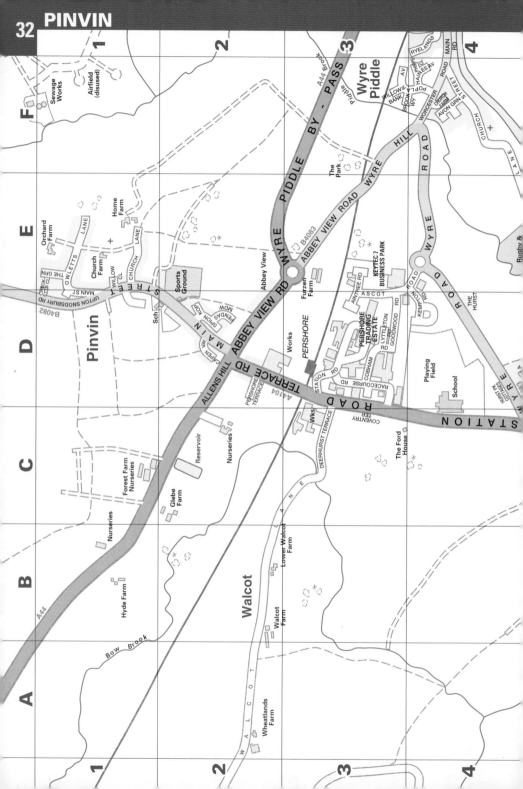

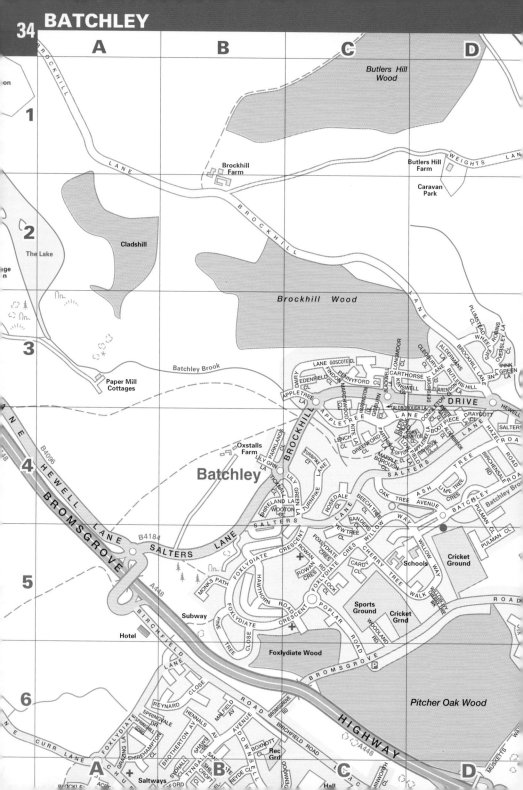

A **B** **C** **D**

1

Butlers Hill Wood

BROCKHILL LANE

WEIGHTS LANE

Brockhill Farm

Butlers Hill Farm

Caravan Park

2

The Lake

Cladshill

BROCKHILL LANE

Brockhill Wood

3

Batchley Brook

Paper Mill Cottages

PLUMSTEAD LA
BROCKHILL LANE
WHEELERS
ROBINS CL
OVERSLEY CL
PINK GREEN LA

LANE GOSCOTE CL
LONGMOOR
CLEOBURY
ALDERMANS LANE
BUTLERS HILL
DAIRY
EDENFIELD CL
PENNYFORD CL
BLACKWELL
CARTHORSE
DEVON
CLARENDON CL
APPLETREE LA
FINDON CL
MARGOTWOOD
GISELLE
ROSWELL
DRIVE
HEWELL
APPLETREE
KITE CL
CORN HAMPTONE
COTTON CL
BOOT PIECE
DRAYCOTT
SALTERS
LENCH CL
GREENFORD CL
COPTON
HAPLEY
FIELD
ALDERBROOK
BOXTREE RD

4

Batchley

HEWELL LANE
BROMSGROVE
B4096
B4184

Oxstalls Farm

BROCKHILL LANE
PARKLANDS
LILY GRN
LILY GREEN LA
SHIRELAND LANE
WOOTON CL
SALTERS
TICKNALL
TURNPIKE

TURNPIKE LANE
ROSEDALE LANE
BEECH TREE CL
OAK TREE CL
MAPPLE BOROUGH
ASH TREE AVENUE
LIME TREE CRES
BIRCHENSALE RD
BATCHLEY Brook
PULMAN CL
PULMAN CL

5

SALTERS LANE
B4184
A448

Subway
Hotel

MONKS PATH
HAWTHORN ROAD
FOXLYDIATE CRESCENT
YEW TREE CL
ROWAN CRES
FOXLYDIATE CRES
SANDERS CL
WILLOW WAY
CARDY CL
CHERRY TREE WALK
Schools

Cricket Ground

FOXLYDIATE CLOSE
PINE TREE
POPLAR ROAD
FOXLYDIATE LOCK CL
Sports Ground
WOODLAND DR
Cricket Grnd

Foxlydiate Wood

P

BIRCHFIELD LANE
BROMSGROVE RD

ROAD

6

REYNARD
SPRINGVALE DR
HENNALS AV
MALFIELD AV
AVENUE ROAD
BROMSGROVE HIGHWAY

Pitcher Oak Wood

CURR LANE
FOXLYDIAT
GRAZING LANE
SHIREHAMPTON
BROTHERTON AV
SHAWS CL
TYNSAL AV
BOXNOTT CL
REYDE CL
Rec Grd
DOWNSDELL
A448

Saltways
Hall
MINWORTH
MUSKETTS WA

A **B** **C** **D**

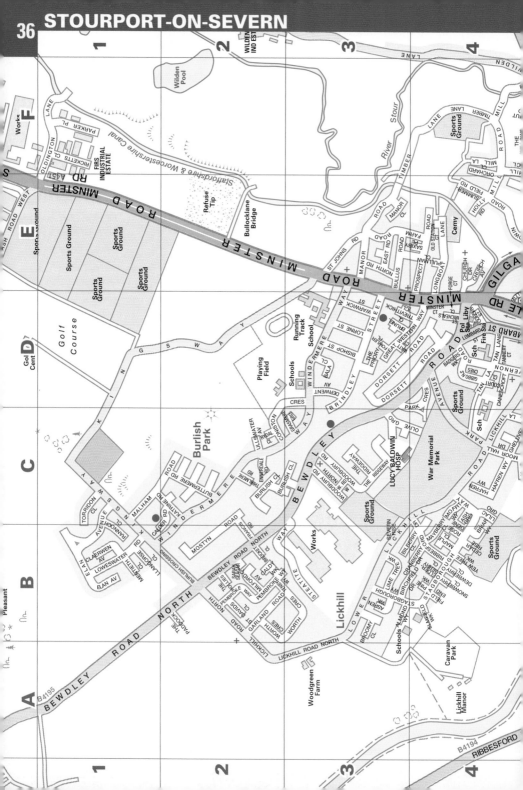

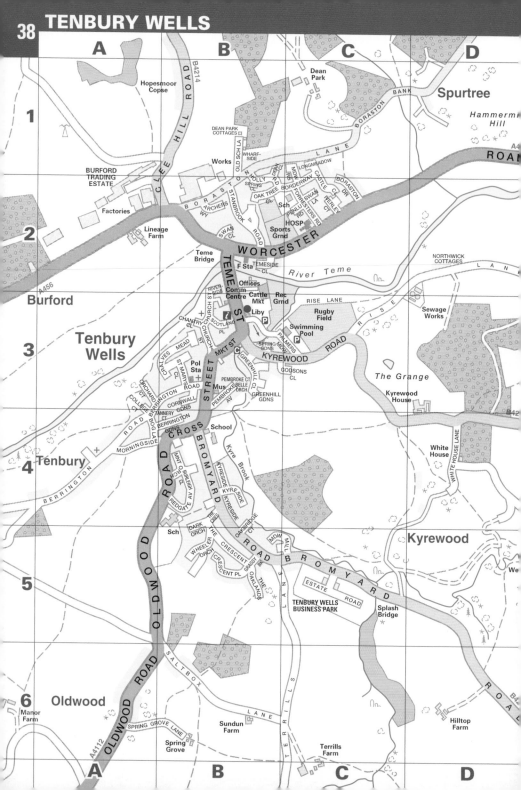

A · **B** · **C** · **D**

Spurtree

Hopesmoor Copse

Hammerm
Hill

B4214

CLEE HILL ROAD

BORASTON BANK

ROA

DEAN PARK COTTAGES

Dean
Park

LANE

A4

Works

WHARF-SIDE

LONGMEADOW

OLD SCH LA

STANBROOK

HOLLY

SPRING

BORDERWAY

CASTLE CT

WERLEY CT

BORASTON DR

NORTHWICK
COTTAGES

BURFORD
TRADING
ESTATE

BORASTON WY

ARCHERS

OAK TREE CL

SWAN CL

Sch

PENBULL RD

FORRESTERS RD LA

SWAN CT

LANE

Factories

Lineage
Farm

SWAN CL

ROAD

Sports Grnd

HOSP

WORCESTER

A456

Teme
Bridge

TEME ST

TEMESIDE CL

TEMESIDE

River Teme

NORTHWICK
COTTAGES

Burford

F Sta

RIVERSIDE

Offices

Comm
Centre

Cattle
Mkt

Rec
Grnd

RISE LANE

Sewage
Works

Tenbury
Wells

SCOTLAND PL

CHURCH ST

Liby

Swimming
Pool

PALMERS MDW

RISE

LANE

CHANTRY CL

MEAD

ST MARY'S RD

MKT ST

SPRING GDNS

KYREWOOD

GODSONS CL

ROAD

The Grange

CRAI LVES

ORCHARD

BERRINGTON

Pol
Sta

CROSS STREET

GREENHILL

Mus

PEMBROKE CT

BELLE ORCH

GREENHILL GDNS

Kyrewood
House

B42

COLLEGE

BOG LA

CORNWALL

TANNERY GDNS

Road

BERRINGTON

GDNS

BROMYARD ROAD

School

Kyre Brook

White
House

WHITE HOUSE LANE

Tenbury

MORNINGSIDE

MINT ORCH

BURLEIGH AV

KYRESIDE

KYRE-SIDE

KYRESIDE

BERRINGTON

REDGATE

THE

OAKBRIDGE CT

Kyrewood

We

Sch

DARK ORCH

WHEELER ORCH

THE CRESCENT

GRASSY DK

MDW

MILL LANE

BROMYARD

TENBURY WELLS
BUSINESS PARK

ESTATE ROAD

Splash
Bridge

ROAD

CRESCENT PL

THE OAKLANDS

OLDWOOD ROAD

SALTBOX

TERRILLS LANE

Oldwood

Manor
Farm

A4112

SPRING GROVE LANE

Spring
Grove

Sundun
Farm

LANE

Terrills
Farm

Hilltop
Farm

B4

ROAD

A · **B** · **C** · **D**

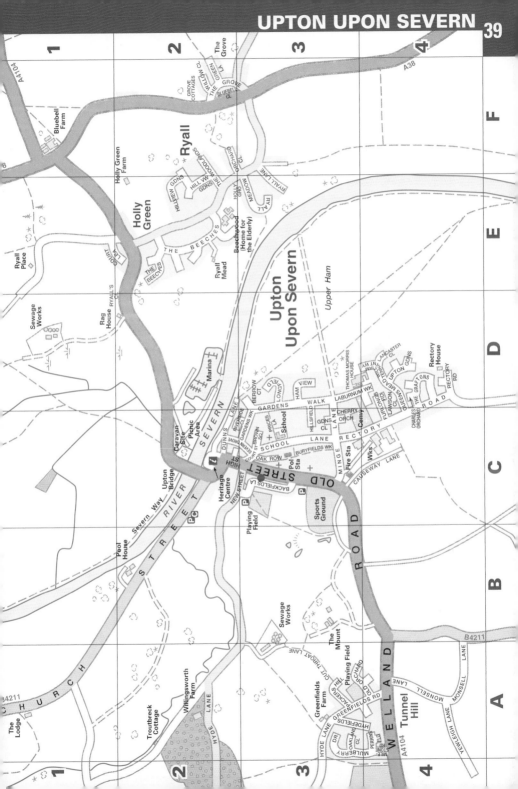

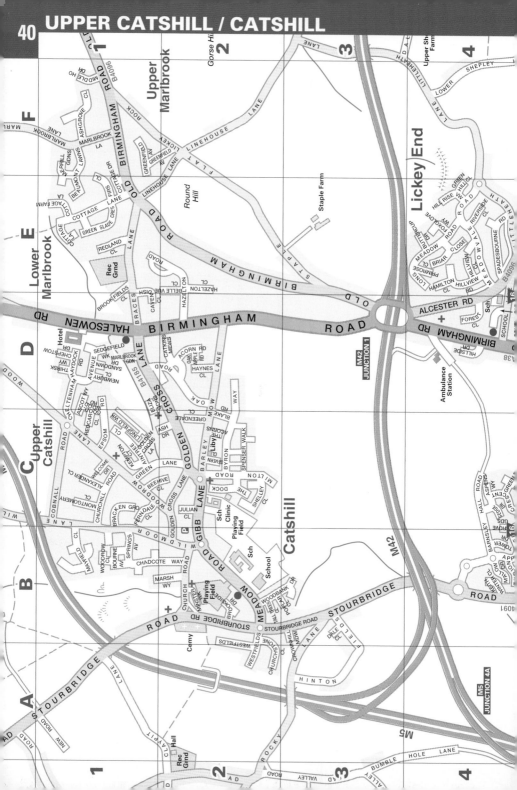

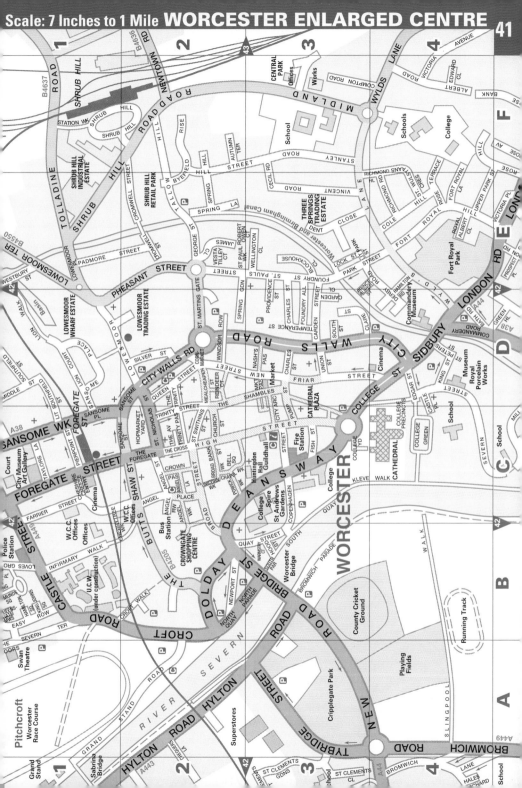

The Index includes some names for which there is insufficient space on the maps. These names are indicated by an * and are followed by the nearest adjoining thoroughfare.

Name	Ref
Cedar Ter B60	17 D5
Cedar Vw B97	35 E4
Cedarwood Gdns WR11	23 F3
Celandine Way WR15	22 C6
Celeste Rd B60	17 F5
Celvestune Way WR9	19 B6
Cemetery La B97	35 E6
Central Pk WR5	41 F3
Central Rd B60	17 E5
Chadbury Rd WR11	20 A3
Chadcote Way B61	40 B1
Chaddesley Gdns DY10	31 G5
Chaddesley Rd DY10	31 G5
Challenger Cl WR14	25 E6
Chalverton Ct WR9	19 A7
Chance La WR14	27 H1
Chancery Mews B60	17 D5
Chantry, Birmingham B47	29 B2
Chantry Cl, Tenbury Wells WR15	38 B3
Chapel Ct DY10	31 H1
Chapel Dr B47	29 B6
Chapel Hill DY10	31 G1
Chapel La B47	29 A6
Chapel Rd B96	13 B2
Chapel St, Bromsgrove B60	16 D4
Chapel St, Evesham WR11	22 D2
Chapel St, Kidderminster DY11	30 D4
Chapel St, Redditch B96	13 B1
Chapel St, Stourbridge DY9	28 C3
Chapel Walk, Bromsgrove B60	16 D4
Chapel Walk, Worcester WR1	41 C2
Charford Rd B60	17 C6
Charity Cres WR11	22 D6
Charlecot Rd WR9	19 E7
Charles Av DY10	31 G1
Charles Cl WR11	22 D4
Charles Dickens Cl WR9	19 C8
Charles Hastings Wall WR4	43 H5
Charles Henry Rd WR9	19 E5
Charles Orchard WR8	39 C4
Charles St, Kidderminster DY10	31 F4
Charles St, Worcester WR1	41 D3
Charles Way WR14	25 F4
Charlock Rd WR14	27 G2
Charlotte Bronte Dr WR9	19 C8
Charlton Cl WR11	22 A3
Charter Pl WR1	41 B1
Chaucer Rd B60	17 F6
Chawson La WR9	19 A7
Chawson Pleck WR9	19 C6
Chawson Rd WR9	19 C6
Cheapside DY13	37 D6
Checketts Cl WR10	32 D1
Chelmsford Dr WR5	43 F5
Cheltenham Av B61	40 C1
Cheltenham Rd, Broadway WR12	13 A6
Cheltenham Rd, Evesham WR11	22 C6
Chepstow Dr B61	40 D1
Chequers Cl, Malvern WR14	25 G2
Chequers Cl, Stourport-on-Severn DY13	37 C7
Chequers La WR2	41 A2
Cherry Cl, Bewdley DY12	14 C4
Cherry Cl, Droitwich Spa WR9	19 F6
Cherry Cl, Evesham WR11	23 F4
Cherry Cl, Offenham WR11	21 F3
Cherry Cres B61	16 B3
Cherry Orchard, Kidderminster DY10	31 F5
Cherry Orchard, Pershore WR10	33 C6
Cherry Orchard, Worcester WR8	39 C3
Cherry Orchard Dr B61	16 B4
Cherry Tree Walk, Redditch B97	34 C5
Cherry Tree Walk, Stourport-on-Severn DY13	37 B8
Cherry Tree Walk, Worcester WR1	41 B1
Cherry Walk B47	29 C4
Cherwell Cl WR4	43 F3
Cheshire Cheese Entry WR1	41 C1
Cheshire Gro DY11	30 B4
Cheshire Av DY13	37 B8
Chesshire Cl DY13	37 B8
Chester Cl WR5	43 G5
Chester Ct WR12	13 B6
Chester Pl WR14	24 C3
Chester Rd North DY10	31 G2
Chester Rd South DY10	31 F6
Chesterton Gdns WR4	43 G4
Chesterwood B47	29 B3
Chestnut Cl WR11	22 B4
Chestnut Cl, Kidderminster DY11	30 C2
Chestnut Cl, Malvern WR14	27 E1
Chestnut Dr WR14	26 D5
Chestnut Gro DY11	30 C2
Chestnut Rd, Bromsgrove B61	16 C2
Chestnut Rd, Redditch B96	13 B2
Chestnut Spinney WR9	19 D7
Chestnut St WR1	42 C3
Chesworth Rd B60	17 F5
Cheviot Cl, Stourport-on-Severn DY13	37 A8
Cheviot Cl, Worcester WR4	43 F3
Chichester Av DY11	30 C1
Childswickham Rd WR12	13 A5
Chiltern Cl, Stourport-on-Severn DY13	37 A8
Chiltern Cl, Worcester WR4	43 F3
Chorley Rd WR9	19 E8
Christ Church Rd WR14	27 E1
Christchurch Rd WR4	43 E3
Church Av DY13	36 E4
Church Cl, Birmingham B47	29 B6
Church Cl, Broadway WR12	13 B6
Church Cl, Worcester WR2	42 A5
Church Ct*, Church St B96	13 B1
Church Dr DY13	36 E4
Church Fm WR10	32 F4
Church Grn East B98	35 F5
Church Grn West B97	35 F5
Church La, Bromsgrove B61	16 C4
Church La, Pershore WR10	32 E1
Church Mews WR12	13 B6
Church Rd, Astwood Bank B96	13 B1
Church Rd, Bromsgrove B61	16 C3
Church Rd, Catshill B61	40 B2
Church Rd, Droitwich Spa WR9	18 E4
Church Rd, Evesham WR11	22 B4
Church Rd, Malvern WR14	24 D3
Church Rd, Redditch B97	35 F5
Church Rd, Worcester WR3	42 D2
Church Row WR10	33 C7
Church St, Broadway WR12	13 B6
Church St, Bromsgrove B61	16 C4
Church St, Evesham WR11	23 E3
Church St, Kidderminster DY10	31 E4
Church St, Malvern WR14	26 D1
Church St, Offenham WR11	21 F3
Church St, Pershore WR10	33 C7
Church St, Stourbridge DY9	28 C2
Church St, Tenbury Wells WR15	38 B3
Church St, Upton Upon Severn WR8	39 A1
Church St, Worcester WR1	41 C2
Church St, Wyre Piddle WR10	32 F4
Church Ter WR2	42 A5
Church Vw DY12	14 D3
Church Walk, Kidderminster DY11	30 D4
Church Walk, Malvern WR14	24 D6
Church Walk, Pershore WR10	33 C7
Church Walk, Stourport-on-Severn DY13	37 B6
Church Walk*, Church St WR15	38 B3
Churchdown Rd WR14	27 F4
Churchfields, Bromsgrove B61	16 C3
Churchfields, Kidderminster DY10	31 E4
Churchfields Gdns B61	16 C3
Churchfields Rd B61	16 C3
Churchill Av WR9	19 C7
Churchill Ct WR11	22 B4
Churchill Dr WR11	25 E1
Churchill Rd B61	40 C1
Churchstone Cl B61	40 A2
Cirencester Cl B60	17 F5
City Arc WR1	41 C3
City Walls Rd WR1	41 D2
Cladsworth Ho*, Lock Cl B97	34 C5
Claerwen Av DY13	36 E1
Claines Cres DY11	31 H5
Clare Rd WR14	25 F6
Clare St WR1	41 D3
Clare Witnell Cl DY11	30 B2
Clarence Cl WR14	26 D1
Clarence Rd WR14	26 D1
Clarence St DY10	31 G4
Clarence Way DY12	15 E2
Clarendon Cl B97	34 D3
Clares Ct DY11	30 D4
Clarks Hill Rise WR14	22 B3
Claughton Ct DY11	30 C6
Claughton St DY11	30 C5
Claverham Cl WR2	42 A6
Clayfield Dr WR14	24 C3
Clayhall Rd WR9	19 E7
Claypit La B61	40 A2
Clayton Dr B60	17 E7
Clee Hill Rd WR15	38 B2
Clee Vw WR9	19 C6
Cleeve Cl DY13	37 A8
Clensmore St DY10	31 E3
Clent Dr DY9	28 E2
Clent Ho*, Burcot La B60	16 E3
Cleobury Cl B97	34 D3
Cleobury Rd DY12	14 B4
Clerkenwell Cres WR14	25 E5
Clifford Cl WR9	19 C8
Clifford Rd WR9	19 C8
Clive Rd, Bromsgrove B60	17 E6
Clive Rd, Redditch B97	35 F4
Clover Way WR14	27 G3
Clyde Av WR11	23 F3
Clydesdale Cl WR9	19 F8
Clydesdale Rd WR9	19 F8
Coates Rd DY10	31 H3
Cobden St DY11	30 D5
Cobham Cl B60	17 C7
Cobham Cres DY12	14 D3
Cobham Ct WR9	19 D5
Cobham Rd, Kidderminster DY10	31 E6
Cobham Rd, Pershore WR10	32 D3
Cobnall Rd B61	40 C1
Cockshot Rd WR14	24 D4
Cockshute Hill WR9	19 F6
Cockshutt La B61	16 A1
Cofton Cl B97	34 C4
Coldicott Gdns WR11	22 C4
Cole Hill WR5	41 E4
Coleford Cl WR9	19 A6
Colege Walk DY10	31 F6
Coleridge Cl WR3	42 C1
College Cl WR15	38 A3
College Grn, Droitwich Spa WR9	19 C6
College Grn, Worcester WR1	41 C4
College Gro WR14	26 D3
College Precincts WR1	41 C4
College Rd, Bromsgrove B60	16 D4
College Rd, Kidderminster DY10	31 F6
College Rd, Malvern WR14	26 D2
College St WR1	41 C3
College Walk B60	16 D4
College Yd WR1	41 C3
Colletts Flds WR12	13 C6
Colletts Gdns WR12	13 C6
Collinghurst Ho*, Backfields La WR8	39 C3
Collinsfield WR11	20 C6
Collis Cl B60	17 B7
Colman Rd WR9	19 D5
Columbine Gro WR11	22 C6
Comberton Av DY10	31 H5
Comberton Ct DY10	31 H6
Comberton Gdns DY10	31 H5
Comberton Hill DY10	31 F5
Comberton Park Rd DY10	31 H6
Comberton Pl DY10	31 F5
Comberton Rd DY10	31 F5
Comberton Ter DY10	31 F5
Comer Av WR2	42 A4
Comer Rd WR2	42 A4
Commandery Rd WR5	41 D4
Common Rd WR11	23 E2
Como Rd WR14	24 D6
Compton Rd WR5	41 F4
Conduit Hill WR11	22 D2
Congleton Cl B97	34 D4
Conifer Gro B61	16 C3
Coningsby Dr DY11	30 B3
Coniston Cl, Bromsgrove B60	17 F5
Coniston Cl, Worcester WR4	43 G2
Coniston Cl WR14	27 G3
Coniston Cres DY13	36 C2
Coniston Way DY12	14 C3
Connaught Rd B60	17 F5
Conningsby Dr WR14	33 A7
Constitution Hill Ringway DY10	31 E6
Conway WR4	43 F3
Conway Dr WR11	23 F3
Conway Rd B60	17 D5
Cooper Cl B60	17 B7
Coopers Cl WR4	43 F1
Coopers Hill B48	12 A3
Coopers La, Evesham WR11	22 D3
Coopers La, Stourport-on-Severn DY13	37 C5
Copcut La WR9	19 A8
Copenhagen St WR1	41 C3
Coppice Cl, Droitwich Spa WR9	18 B3
Coppice Cl, Malvern WR14	24 C1
Coppice Cl, Redditch B97	35 E5
Coppice Way WR9	18 B3
Copsewood Av WR4	43 H4
Copthorn Ho*, Burcot Rd B60	16 E3
Corbett Av WR9	19 D6
Corbett Cl B60	17 F6
Corbett Rd, Birmingham B47	29 B2
Corbett Rd, Kidderminster DY11	30 B2
Corbett St WR9	19 D6
Cordle Marsh Rd DY12	15 F1
Corn Mill Rd WR11	22 C5
Cornfield Av B60	17 B8
Cornhampton Cl B97	34 D4
Cornmarket WR1	41 D2
Cornmore WR10	33 B8
Cornwall Av DY11	30 D1
Cornwall Gdns WR15	38 B3
Coronation Rd WR14	25 F2
Coronation St WR11	23 F2
Coronation Ter B60	17 E7
Coronation Way DY10	31 H5
Corporation St DY10	31 E5
Cotland WR3	42 D1
Cotswold Av WR14	33 A7
Cotswold Rd WR14	25 F6
Cotswold Vw*, Mill St WR11	22 D2
Cotswold Way B60	16 D1
Cottage Dr B60	40 E1
Cottage Farm La B60	40 E1
Cottage La B60	40 E1
Cotton Pool Rd B61	16 B4
Counting House Way B60	17 B8
Country Wide Trading Est WR4	**43 E4**
Court Cl, Kidderminster DY11	30 C1
Court Cl, Stourport-on-Severn DY13	36 D4
Court Gdns WR14	27 E1
Court La WR11	21 F3
Court Lea WR8	39 E2
Court Rd WR14	27 E2
Court Sq B98	35 G5
Court St WR8	39 C3
Coventry Highway B98	35 H4
Coventry St DY10	31 F4
Coventry Ter WR10	32 C3
Cover Grn WR4	43 H3
Covercroft WR9	19 D5
Cowl St WR11	22 D2
Cowleigh Bank WR14	24 B3
Cowleigh Rd WR14	24 A3
Coxlea Cl WR11	22 C1
Coxwell Dr WR14	25 F4
Crab Apple Way WR11	23 F4
Crabtree Cl DY9	28 D1
Crabtree Ct B61	16 B3
Crabtree Dr B61	16 C3
Crabtree La B61	16 B3
Cralves Mead WR15	38 B3
Cranberry Dr DY13	36 B3
Crane St DY11	30 D4
Crescent Pl WR15	38 B5
Crescent Rd DY11	30 D5
Crestwood Av DY11	30 B5
Croft Bank WR14	24 A6
Croft Farm Dr WR14	24 A6

Croft Gdns WR12 13 B6
Croft Rd, Evesham WR11 20 C6
Croft Rd, Worcester WR1 41 B2
Croft Walk WR1 41 B2
Croftdown Ct WR14 26 C1
Crofters Cl WR9 18 B2
Crofters End WR9 18 B2
Crofters Grn WR9 18 B2
Crofters Hill WR9 18 B2
Crofters Way WR9 18 B3
Cromwell Ct WR14 25 E3
Cromwell Rd WR14 25 E3
Cromwell St WR1 41 E2
Cropthorne Dr B47 29 D2
Cross Keys Mews DY9 28 B4
Cross St WR15 38 B4
Crossley Pk DY11 31 E4
Crossley Walk B60 17 B7
Crown Cl B61 16 D4
Crown La DY10 31 E4
Crown Lea Av WR14 27 G1
Crown Mdw B48 12 C3
Crown Pass WR1 41 C2
Crown St WR3 42 B1
Crowngate Shopping Centre WR1 41 B2
Crownhill Mdw B61 40 A3
Crowther St DY11 30 D4
Crundalls La DY12 15 E1
Crutch La WR9 18 E2
Cumberland St WR1 42 B2
Curr La B97 34 A6
Cut Throat La WR8 39 A3
Cutty Sark Dr DY13 37 E6
Cygnet Cl B48 12 C2
Cypress Cl WR11 23 F5
Cypress Ct DY10 31 G6
Cyprus Av B96 13 B1
Cyril Rd WR3 42 D2

Dagnell End Rd B98 35 F1
Dairy La B97 34 C3
Dalbury Cl WR14 24 D3
Dale Cl B61 40 B3
Dale Rd B98 35 G4
Damson Way DY12 15 F2
Danebury Pk WR14 24 B4
Danes Cl WR14 25 F3
Danescroft Dr B97 36 D4
Danford Rd B47 29 B3
Danube Cl WR9 19 B7
Dark La, Birmingham B47 29 A2
Dark La, Bromsgrove B60 17 B8
Dark La, Redditch B96 13 A2
Dark Orchard WR15 38 B5
Dart Rd WR5 43 F4
Darwin Av WR4 43 G4
Daston Cl WR12 13 C5
Daty Croft WR4 43 H1
Davenham Cl WR14 25 E6
Davenham Rd B60 17 F5
Davenport Dr B60 17 E5
Davies Rd WR11 22 C5
Dawson Rd B61 16 B4
Daybrook Cl B97 34 D4
De La Bere Cl WR11 22 D2
De Salis Ct WR9 18 B1
De Salis Dr WR9 18 B1
De Walden Rd WR14 26 A1
Deacle Pl WR11 23 F2
Dean Cl WR15 38 B1
Dean Park Cotts WR15 38 B1
Deansway, Bromsgrove B61 17 B5
Deansway, Worcester WR1 41 C2
Debdale Av WR4 43 H2
Dee Way WR4 43 F3
Deerhurst Ter WR10 32 C3
Defford Rd WR10 33 A8
Delamere Rd, Bewdley DY12 15 F2
Delamere Rd, Malvern WR14 25 E6

Dellow Gro B48 12 C4
Delphinium Cl DY11 30 D1
Denison Cl WR14 25 F5
Dent Cl WR5 41 E3
Derby Rd WR5 41 D4
Dereham Cl DY11 24 D4
Derwent Av DY13 36 D3
Derwent Cl WR4 43 F1
Derwent Dr DY12 14 C2
Derwent Gro WR9 19 B7
Derwent Way B60 17 E5
Devon Cl DY11 30 D1
Devon Dr WR14 25 G6
Devon Rd WR5 43 F6
Devonport Cl B97 34 D3
Dewberry Cl DY13 36 B4
Dewsbury Cl B96 13 B2
Digby Rd WR11 23 F3
Diglis Av WR1 42 C6
Diglis Rd WR5 42 C6
Discovery Rd DY13 37 E4
Dixie Ct WR14 24 C4
Dixon St DY10 31 E5
Dodford Ho*, Burcot La B60 16 E3
Doebank Dr B96 13 B2
Dog La DY12 15 E3
Dog Lane Mews*, Dog La DY12 15 E3
Dogwood Cl WR14 25 G4
Dolday WR1 41 B2
Dolphin Rd B98 35 H3
Domar Rd DY11 30 B3
Don Rd WR4 43 F3
Donney Brook WR11 17 C6
Dorsett Rd DY13 36 D3
Douglas Rd B47 29 B2
Dove Cl WR4 43 F3
Dovecote Rd, Bromsgrove B61 17 B5
Dovecote Rd, Droitwich Spa WR9 19 E7
Doverdale Av DY10 31 H5
Doverdale Cl WR9 19 C6
Doverdale La WR9 18 A1
Dowles Cft WR9 18 C4
Dowles Rd DY12 14 C1
Downsell Rd B97 34 B6
Dragoon Flds B60 17 F6
Drake Cres DY11 30 A3
Drakes Cross Par B47 29 B4
Drakes Lea WR11 23 E1
Draycott Cl B97 34 D4
Drayton Ct B60 17 E6
Drovers Grn WR9 18 C3
Drovers Pl WR9 18 C3
Drovers Walk DY10 31 F5
Drovers Way, Bromsgrove B60 17 B7
Drovers Way, Droitwich Spa WR9 18 C3
Drummond Rd B60 17 F6
Dry Mill La DY12 14 B1
Duck Mdw WR4 43 H2
Dudley St DY10 31 E4
Dugard Way DY11 31 G1
Dugdale Dr WR4 43 H4
Duke of Edinburgh Way WR14 25 F2
Duke Pl DY10 31 E3
Dukes Way WR14 27 F3
Dunhampton Dr DY10 31 H1
Dunley Gdns DY13 37 B6
Dunley Rd DY13 37 A7
Dunnington Av DY10 31 G1
Dunns La WR8 39 C2
Durcott La WR11 23 E3
Durcott Rd WR11 23 E3
Durham Cl B61 16 C3
Durham Rd WR5 43 G4
Dutton St WR3 42 D3
Dyas Rd B47 29 C2

Early River Pl DY12 14 C3
Easemore Rd B98 35 F5
East Park Dr WR9 18 B4

East Rd, Bromsgrove B60 17 E5
East Rd, Stourport-on-Severn DY13 36 E3
East St, Kidderminster DY10 31 F4
East St, Worcester WR1 42 C3
Eastabrook Cl WR14 24 D2
Eastern Hill B96 13 B1
Easthope Cl DY13 37 C7
Easton Gro B47 29 C2
Eastward Rd WR14 24 D1
Eastwick WR1 22 C4
Eastwood Dr DY10 31 H6
Eastwood Rd WR1 42 D2
Easy Row WR1 41 B1
Eaton Rd WR14 26 C5
Ebrington Rd WR14 24 A5
Echells Cl B61 16 B4
Eddy Rd DY10 31 F3
Edenfield Cl B97 34 C3
Edgar St WR1 41 D4
Edgioake La B96 13 B3
Edinburgh Cl DY10 31 E3
Edith Berry Ct WR14 25 F6
Edith Walk WR14 24 C6
Ednall La B60 17 D5
Edward Cl WR5 41 F4
Edward St, Evesham WR11 22 C2
Edward St, Redditch B97 35 E5
Edwin Cres B60 17 C6
Elan Av DY13 36 B1
Elan Cl DY13 14 C3
Elbury Park Rd WR4 43 G3
Elderberry Cl DY13 36 B4
Elgar Av WR14 25 F5
Elgar Cres WR9 19 D8
Elgar Ct WR3 42 D3
Eliot Ct WR14 25 E5
Eliza Gdns B61 40 D1
Elizabeth Av WR9 19 F5
Elizabeth Rd WR11 22 D4
Elizabeth Way B97 35 E4
Ellenbrook Cl B97 34 C4
Ellesmere Dr DY12 14 C3
Ellis Rd WR2 42 A6
Elm Ct B97 35 E5
Elm Gro, Bromsgrove B61 16 E2
Elm Gro, Stourport-on-Severn DY13 37 B8
Elm Rd, Evesham WR11 23 E3
Elm Rd, Kidderminster DY10 31 G4
Elm Rd, Redditch B97 35 E4
Elm Rd, Worcester WR2 42 A4
Elmfield Gdns WR5 42 D6
Elmfield Walk DY13 36 B4
Elmley Cl WR14 25 F6
Elmley Ho*, Cardy Cl B97 34 C5
Elmside WR11 23 F3
Elmwood Gro B47 29 B3
Elsh Gate DY13 14 D3
Elton Rd DY12 14 C3
Ely Cl, Kidderminster DY11 30 B4
Ely Cl, Worcester WR5 43 G5
Emes Cl WR10 33 B7
Emporer Pl DY10 31 F2
Endeavor Pl DY13 37 E6
Enfield Ind Est B97 35 F3
Engadine Cl WR14 27 E4
Engine La DY13 37 D5
Enid Blyton Cnr WR9 19 D8
Ennerdale Dr WR4 43 G2
Ennerdale Rd DY13 36 C2
Enterprise Way WR11 23 F6
Epsom Rd B61 40 C1
Erica Cl DY11 30 D1
Erneley Cl DY13 37 C6
Eskdale Cl WR4 43 F2

Estate Rd WR15 38 C5
Eston Av WR14 27 G1
Eton Walk DY9 28 C1
Etonhurst WR14 27 F1
Evendine Rd WR11 22 A3
Eversley Cl WR14 25 F5
Eversley Gro WR14 25 F5
Evertons Cl WR9 19 C7
Evesham By-Pass WR11 23 E6
Evesham Ho*, Burcot Rd B60 16 E3
Evesham Rd, Offenham WR11 21 G5
Evesham Rd, Pershore WR10 33 D8
Evesham Rd, Redditch B96 13 B1
Evesham Rd, Twyford WR11 20 C3
Evesham St B97 35 F6
Exchange St DY10 31 E5
Exeter Cl DY11 30 A4
Exeter Rd WR5 43 G4
Exmoor Dr B61 16 D2

Fabricus Av WR9 19 D6
Factory La B61 17 C5
Fairfax Ct WR2 42 A5
Fairfield DY10 31 G5
Fairfield Cl WR4 43 F1
Fairfield Ho*, Burcot La B60 16 E3
Fairfield Pl WR11 22 C4
Fairfield Rd WR11 22 C4
Fairmont Rd B60 17 E6
Fairoak Dr B60 17 C7
Fairwater Cl WR11 23 E3
Fairways WR10 33 C6
Fairways Cl DY10 31 G6
Fairways Walk WR10 33 C6
Falcon Cl WR9 19 F8
Falkland Rd WR11 23 F5
Fallowfields Cl B61 16 B3
Falstaff Av B47 29 B3
Falstaff Dr WR9 19 C7
Farleigh Rd WR10 33 B8
Farley Rd WR14 25 E3
Farm Rd, Redditch B98 35 H6
Farm Rd, Stourport-on-Severn DY13 36 E4
Farmers Ct WR9 18 B3
Farmers Grn WR9 18 B3
Farmers Piece*, Farmers Way WR9 18 B3
Farmers Rd B60 17 C7
Farmers Way WR9 18 B3
Farncombe Ter WR10 33 B8
Farrier Cl B60 17 B7
Farrier St WR1 41 C1
Farriers Cl WR9 18 B4
Farriers Cnr WR9 18 B4
Farriers Sq WR9 18 B4
Farriers Way WR9 18 B4
Farthing La B97 34 C4
Farundles Av WR4 43 H2
Feckenham Ho*, Burcot La B60 16 E3
Feckenham Rd B96 13 B1
Fen Cl DY10 31 E2
Fenton Rd B47 29 C2
Ferndale Cl, Bromsgrove B61 40 C1
Ferndale Cl, Stourbridge DY9 28 C3
Ferndale Cl, Stourport-on-Severn DY13 37 F5
Ferndale Cres DY11 37 F5
Ferney Hill Av B97 35 E6
Fernhill Gro WR14 25 E6
Ferry La WR11 21 F4
Ferry Villas WR2 42 B1
Ferry Vw WR11 22 C3
Field Cl B60 17 B8
Field End DY13 36 B4
Field La DY9 28 E3

Field Ter WR5 42 C6
Fielden Cl WR11 23 E3
Fieldfare Cl WR14 24 B1
Fieldways Cl B47 29 B2
Findon Cl B97 34 C3
Findon St DY10 31 F4
Finstall Rd B60 17 F6
Fir Tree Cl B97 35 E4
Fir Way WR4 43 E1
Fircroft Rd B60 17 A8
Firenze Rd B60 17 F6
Firs Cl, Bromsgrove B60 40 E1
Firs Cl, Malvern WR14 26 D3
Firs Ind Est DY13 36 F1
Fish Hill B98 35 F4
Fish St WR1 41 C3
Fishing Line Rd B98 35 F4
Five Oaks Cl WR14 27 G1
Flag Meadow Walk WR1 42 C2
Flavel Rd B60 17 C7
Flax Cl B47 29 C4
Fleece Rd WR12 13 B5
Florence Av WR9 19 C7
Fockbury Mill La B61 16 B1
Foley Ter WR14 26 C1
Ford Cl WR14 27 G1
Ford La WR9 18 E2
Ford Rd B61 17 C5
Fordhouse Rd B60 17 E5
Foregate St, Redditch B96 13 B1
Foregate St, Worcester WR1 41 C1
Forelands Gro B61 17 B6
Forest Cl, Bewdley DY12 14 D3
Forest Cl, Bromsgrove B60 40 D4
Forest Gate WR11 23 E5
Forest Way B47 29 C3
Forge Ct DY13 36 E4
Forge Dr B61 16 C3
Forge Mill Rd B98 35 G3
Forresters Rd WR15 38 C2
Fort Mahon Pl DY12 14 D3
Fort Royal Ct WR4 43 E6
Fort Royal Hill WR5 41 E4
Fort Royal WR5 41 E4
Forward Cotts B48 12 B4
Foster Rd WR11 23 E4
Fosters Cnr*, Dog La DY12 15 E3
Foundry Alley WR1 41 D3
Foundry St, Stourport-on-Severn DY13 36 D4
Foundry St, Worcester WR1 41 E3
Fountain Cl WR11 22 C4
Fountain Gdns WR11 22 C4
Fountain Pl WR1 42 B2
Four Pools Ind Est WR11 22 D5
Four Pools La WR11 23 E6
Four Pools Rd WR11 23 E4
Fowler Pl DY13 36 D3
Fox La B61 17 B6
Foxglove Cl, Evesham WR11 23 F5
Foxglove Cl, Malvern WR14 27 G2
Foxglove Way B60 40 E4
Foxhunter Cl WR9 19 F8
Foxlydiate Cres B97 34 B5
Foxlydiate La B97 34 A6
Foxwalks Av B61 17 B6
Franche Court Dr DY11 30 C1
Franche Rd DY11 30 C2
Franchise St DY11 30 D6
Francis Rd, Bromsgrove B60 17 C7
Francis Rd, Stourport-on-Severn DY13 36 B2
Frank Freeman Ct DY10 31 F2
Fraser Cl WR14 27 E3
Frederick Rd WR14 24 D3

Entry	Ref
Hillside Cl, Worcester WR5	43 F4
Hillside Dr, Bromsgrove B61	40 D4
Hillside Dr, Kidderminster DY11	30 A3
Hilltop Av DY12	15 G2
Hillview Cl B60	40 E4
Hillview Dr WR4	24 C3
Hillview Rd B60	40 E4
Hilton Rd WR14	27 G2
Hingley Av WR4	43 H3
Hinton Av B48	12 C3
Hinton Flds B61	40 A3
Hither Green La B98	35 G2
Hoarstone DY8	28 B2
Hoarstone Cl DY12	15 F1
Hoarstone La DY12	15 G1
Hock Coppice WR4	43 H3
Hodfar Rd DY13	37 E7
Holloway WR10	33 A6
Holloway Dr, Pershore WR10	33 A6
Holloway Dr, Redditch B98	35 G6
Holloway La B98	35 G5
Holloway Pk B98	35 H6
Holly Cl, Droitwich Spa WR9	19 E8
Holly Cl, Evesham WR11	23 F5
Holly Ct DY10	31 E2
Holly Dr B47	29 D2
Holly Gro, Bromsgrove B61	16 C3
Holly Gro, Worcester WR8	39 E2
Holly Mount Rd WR4	43 E2
Holly Mt WR4	43 E2
Holly Rd, Stourport-on-Severn DY13	36 E4
Holly Rd, Tenbury Wells WR15	38 B2
Holly Rd B61	16 C3
Hollywood By-Pass B47	29 A2
Hollywood Dr B47	29 C1
Hollywood Gdns B47	29 B1
Hollywood La B47	29 C1
Holman St DY11	30 D6
Holmcroft Rd DY10	31 H5
Holmwood Av DY11	30 B4
Holmwood Dr B97	35 E5
Holmwood Gdns WR11	23 E5
Holywell Hill WR2	42 A3
Home Piece WR9	19 B6
Homefield Rd WR2	42 A6
Homestead WR9	19 C6
Homfray Rd DY10	31 G2
Honeybrook Gdns DY11	30 C1
Honeybrook La DY11	30 C1
Honeybrook Ter*, Honeybrook DY11	30 C1
Honeychurch Cl B98	35 G6
Honeysuckle Cl WR11	22 D6
Honister Dr WR4	43 G1
Hoo Rd DY10	31 F6
Hood St WR1	41 B3
Hoopers La B96	13 B2
Hop Pole La DY12	14 C3
Hopgardens Av B60	16 E4
Hopmarket Yd WR1	41 C2
Hornbeam Cl DY12	14 C4
Hornbeam Ho DY12	14 C3
Hornyold Av WR14	24 C4
Hornyold Rd WR14	24 C4
Horse Fair DY11	31 F3
Hospital Bank WR14	24 C4
Hospital Rd WR14	24 B1
Houle Cl DY11	30 C4
Houndsfield Cl B47	29 D3
Houndsfield Ct B47	29 C4
Houndsfield Gro B47	29 B4
Houndsfield La B47	29 B4
Housman Cl B60	17 B6
Housman Ct*, Housman Pk B60	16 D4
Housman Pk B60	16 D4
Howard Av B61	16 B3
Howsell Rd WR14	24 D3
Huband Cl B98	35 H3
Hudson Cl WR10	33 B6
Huins Cl B98	35 H5
Humber Rd WR5	43 F4
Hume St DY11	30 D5
Humphrey Av B60	17 C7
Hunter Rise WR10	33 B7
Hunters Cl WR9	18 B4
Hunters End WR9	18 B4
Hunters Grn WR9	18 B4
Hunters Pl WR9	18 B4
Hunters Way WR9	18 B4
Hurcott Ct DY10	31 G3
Hurcott Rd DY10	31 F3
Hurst Park Cotts WR10	32 D4
Hurst Rd WR10	33 C5
Huxleys Way WR11	22 C2
Huxtable Rise WR4	43 H3
Hyde Cl B60	16 F4
Hyde La, Worcester WR8	39 A2
Hyde La, Worcester WR8	39 A3
Hydefields WR8	39 A4
Hylton Rd WR2	41 A2
Hylton Rd WR11	22 A3
Ilkley Cl WR4	43 G2
Imperial Av DY10	31 G2
Imperial Gro DY10	31 G2
Imperial Rd WR14	27 E1
Inches La WR11	22 D1
Inett Way WR9	19 A5
Ingles Dr WR2	42 A5
Ingram Cres DY12	14 D2
Ipsley St B98	35 F6
Ironside Cl DY12	14 C4
Isaacs Way WR9	19 D8
Isbourne Cres WR11	22 D2
Ismere Way DY10	31 G1
Isobel Harris Gdns WR14	25 F2
Iverley Ct WR15	38 C2
Ivor Rd B97	35 E6
Ivy Ct WR11	23 F2
Ivy St WR3	42 B1
Jackdaw La WR9	19 F8
Jackson Cres DY13	37 C7
Jamaica Cres WR14	26 C5
Jamaica Rd WR14	24 D3
James Cl WR1	41 E2
James Rd DY10	31 H2
Jasmine Gro B61	16 C2
Jasmine Rd WR14	26 C5
Jasmine Walk WR11	22 C5
Jays Cres B48	12 D1
Jellyman Cl DY11	30 C4
Jerusalem Walk DY10	31 H3
Jill La B96	13 C1
Jinnah Rd B98	35 G6
Johnson Cl B98	35 H4
Jordan Cl DY11	30 B5
Jordan Ct*, Dog La DY12	15 E3
Jordens Walk DY12	15 F2
Jubilee Dr WR14	26 B6
Julian Cl B61	40 C2
Junction Rd B61	16 B3
Juniper Ct DY10	31 G6
Juniper Pl DY10	31 G6
Juniper Way WR14	26 C5
Katrine Rd DY13	36 C2
Keats Pl DY10	31 H4
Keele Cl WR4	43 E3
Keil Cl WR12	13 B6
Keith Winter Cl B61	16 D1
Kelvin Cl DY11	30 B3
Kemerton Ho*, Cherry Tree Walk B97	34 C5
Kempton Cl WR11	22 C4
Kempton Ct B61	40 C1
Kempton Rd WR10	32 D4
Kendal Cl B60	17 E5
Kendal Grn WR4	43 H1
Kendal St WR3	42 D3
Kendlewood Rd DY10	31 H1
Kenilworth Cl WR3	42 D3
Kennel La WR12	13 B6
Kennet Grn WR5	43 E4
Kent Cl, Evesham WR11	22 B3
Kent Cl, Malvern WR14	25 F1
Kentmere Cl WR4	43 G1
Kentmere Rd B60	17 F5
Kenway B47	29 C2
Kenwood Av WR4	43 F2
Kenwood Cl WR4	43 F3
Kenyon Cl B60	17 D5
Keplax Gdns WR3	42 A1
Kerry Hill B60	17 C8
Kerswell Cl B97	34 C3
Keswick Dr WR4	43 G1
Keytec 7 Bsns Pk WR10	**32 E3**
Kidderminster Rd, Bewdley DY12	15 E3
Kidderminster Rd, Bromsgrove B61	16 A4
Kidderminster Rd, Droitwich Spa WR9	18 B1
Kidderminster Rd, Stourbridge DY9	28 C3
Kidderminster Rd South DY9	28 B4
King Charles Cl DY11	30 D4
King Charles Ct*, Bewdley WR11	22 D2
King Edmunds Sq WR1	41 B1
King Edward Av B61	16 C2
King Edward Rd B61	16 C1
King Edwards Rd WR14	26 C5
King George Av, Bromsgrove B61	16 C2
King George Av, Droitwich Spa WR9	19 D6
King George Cl B61	16 C2
King Georges Way WR10	33 C6
King Johns Sq WR1	41 B1
King St WR1	41 D4
Kingfisher Ct, Birmingham B48	12 C2
Kingfisher Ct, Droitwich Spa WR9	18 E4
Kings Arms La DY13	37 B8
Kings Ct WR4	43 H4
Kings La WR11	20 B1
Kings Rd, Evesham WR11	23 E3
Kings Rd, Kidderminster DY11	30 D4
Kingsdale Ct WR12	13 C5
Kingshill Cl WR14	25 E6
Kingsley Av WR8	35 H5
Kingston Cl WR9	19 E7
Kingsway DY13	36 B1
Kingswood Rd WR9	18 A1
Kinnersley Rd WR14	24 C1
Kinver Cl DY9	28 E1
Kipling Cl WR14	25 E5
Kirkstone Dr WR4	43 G2
Kite La B97	34 C4
Kleve Walk WR1	41 C3
Knapp Way WR14	24 C3
Knoll La WR14	27 F3
Knowesley Cl B60	17 F3
Knowledge Cotts WR11	21 F4
Kylemilne Way DY13	37 F5
Kyreside WR15	38 B4
Kyrewood Rd WR15	38 B3
Lakes Cl DY11	30 D3
Lakes Ct DY12	14 C3
Lamb Bank WR14	24 B4
Lambourne Av WR14	25 E2
Lambourne Dr DY12	14 C2
Lancaster Cl WR8	39 D4
Lancaster Rd DY12	14 D3
Lancelott Ct WR10	33 B6
Land Oak Dr DY10	31 H1
Lane End Walk DY13	37 C7
Lanesfield Pk WR11	20 C6
Laneside Gdns DY12	14 C3
Langdale Cl WR4	43 G1
Langdale Dr WR4	43 G1
Langdale Rd, Stourport-on-Severn DY13	37 A7
Langdale Rd, Worcester WR3	42 B2
Langland Av WR14	25 F5
Langland Cl WR14	25 F6
Langley Rd WR9	19 E7
Lansdown Grn DY11	30 C5
Lansdowne Cl WR14	25 F6
Lansdowne Cres, Malvern WR14	25 E6
Lansdowne Cres, Worcester WR3	42 D2
Lansdowne Cres La WR3	42 D2
Lansdowne Mews WR11	23 E3
Lansdowne Rd, Malvern WR14	24 D3
Lansdowne Rd, Worcester WR3	42 C2
Lansdowne St WR1	42 C2
Lansdowne Ter, Malvern WR14	25 E6
Lansdowne Ter, Worcester WR1	42 C2
Lansdowne Walk WR3	42 C2
Lapal Cl WR2	42 A5
Larch Rd, Evesham WR11	23 E5
Larch Rd, Worcester WR4	43 E3
Larchfield Cl WR14	24 C3
Larford Walk DY13	37 C7
Lark Hill WR5	43 E6
Lark Mews WR9	19 F8
Larkhill DY10	31 F3
Larkhill Rd WR5	43 E6
Larkspur Dr WR11	22 C6
Laslett St WR3	42 D2
Latimer Rd B48	12 C4
Laurel Av WR11	23 F4
Laurel Cl B98	35 F6
Laurel Gro B61	16 C2
Laurel Rd WR4	43 E2
Laurels Av WR11	21 G5
Laurels Rd WR11	21 F4
Laurelwood Cl WR9	19 F8
Laurelwood Rd WR9	19 F8
Lavender Dr WR3	42 B1
Lavender Walk, Evesham WR11	22 C6
Lavender Walk, Malvern WR14	27 G2
Lawnside WR14	26 D1
Lawnside Cl*, Perrins Fld WR8	39 A4
Lawson Cl WR8	39 C4
Lax La DY12	15 E3
Laxton Dr DY12	14 C3
Layamon Walk DY13	37 C6
Layton Av WR14	25 F4
Lea Bank Av DY11	30 B5
Lea Castle Cl DY10	31 G1
Lea Green La B47	29 D3
Lea Park Rise B61	16 D1
Lea St DY10	31 G5
Lea Wood Gro DY11	30 B5
Leadbetter Dr B61	16 B4
Leadon Rd WR14	27 H1
Leahill Cl WR14	24 C5
Leamington Rd WR12	13 B4
Leasowes Rd WR14	21 F4
Lechmere Cres WR14	24 D2
Ledbury Ho*, Cardy Cl B97	34 C5
Ledwich Cl WR9	19 C5
Ledwych Gdns WR9	19 C5
Ledwych Rd WR9	18 C4
Lee Rd B47	29 C2
Leicester Gro WR11	22 D1
Leicester St WR1	42 B2
Leigh Gro WR9	18 C4
Leigh Sinton Rd WR14	24 C1
Lench Cl B97	34 C4
Lenchville WR10	31 G1
Leonard Av DY10	31 H1
Leopard Rise WR5	43 H4
Leswell La DY10	31 F4
Leswell Rd DY10	31 F4
Leswell St DY10	31 F4
Leycroft WR9	19 F7
Leys Walk WR11	23 E2
Lichfield Av, Evesham WR11	23 F2
Lichfield Av, Kidderminster DY11	30 A4
Lichfield Av, Worcester WR5	43 G4
Lichfield St DY13	37 D5
Lickey Rock B60	40 F2
Lickhill Rd DY13	36 C4
Lickhill Rd North DY13	36 A2
Lifford Gdns WR12	13 A6
Lilac Av WR4	43 E3
Lilac Cl, Droitwich Spa WR9	19 F8
Lilac Cl, Evesham WR11	22 B4
Lilac Gro DY13	36 C4
Lily Green La B97	34 B4
Lime Av WR4	43 E1
Lime Cl B47	29 C4
Lime Ct DY10	31 G6
Lime Gro B61	16 D2
Lime St WR11	23 E2
Lime Tree Av, Broadway WR12	13 C5
Lime Tree Av, Malvern WR14	26 C5
Lime Tree Cres B97	34 A4
Lime Tree Walk DY13	36 B3
Lincoln Cres DY11	30 A4
Lincoln Grn WR5	43 F5
Lincoln Rd B61	16 C2
Linden Av, Kidderminster DY10	31 G4
Linden Av, Stourport-on-Severn DY13	37 B7
Linden Cl WR11	23 F5
Linden Gdns DY10	31 H4
Linden Gro DY10	31 G4
Linden Rd WR4	43 F2
Lindsey Av WR11	23 E3
Linehouse La B60	40 E1
Lingfield Rd, Bewdley DY12	15 G1
Lingfield Rd, Evesham WR11	22 C4
Lingfield Walk B61	40 C1
Link Rd WR11	22 D5
Link Ter WR14	24 C5
Link Way WR14	25 E3
Linksview Cres WR5	43 G5
Lion Ct WR1	41 D1
Lion Hill DY13	37 D5
Lion St DY10	31 F4
Lion Walk WR1	41 D1
Little Chestnut Cl WR14	42 C3
Little Grange Cotts*, Cleobury Rd B97	14 C3
Little Hill WR9	19 B6
Little Hill Ct WR9	19 B6
Little Hill Grn WR9	19 A6
Little London WR1	42 B2
Little Orchard WR9	19 C6
Little Park WR9	19 C6
Little Park St WR5	41 E3
Little Penny Rope WR10	33 B8
Little Priest La WR10	33 C7
Little Southfield St WR1	41 C1
Littleheath La B60	40 E4

Littleshaw Cft B47 29 D5
Littleshaw La B47 29 D5
Littleworth St WR11 22 D2
Littleworth Walk WR11 22 C2
Liverpool Rd WR5 43 F5
Llangorse Cl DY13 36 B1
Llewellyn Cl DY13 37 F8
Lloyd Cl WR11 20 C1
Load St DY12 15 E3
Lobelia Cl DY11 30 D1
Lock Cl B97 34 C5
Lock St WR5 41 E3
Lodge Cl DY12 15 F2
Lodge Cotts DY13 37 D5
Lodge Cres DY9 28 C2
Lodge Dr WR14 24 C5
Lodge Rd, Redditch B98 35 G5
Lodge Rd, Stourport-on-Severn DY13 37 D5
Lombard St DY13 36 D4
London La*, High St WR8 39 C2
London Rd WR5 41 D4
Long Acre DY10 31 F3
Long Cl DY9 28 B3
Long Compton Dr DY9 28 C2
Long Hedger WR10 33 A8
Long Meadow Rd B60 40 E4
Long Sling WR9 19 C7
Longbank DY12 14 A5
Longboat La DY13 36 E4
Longfield WR8 39 D3
Longmeadow WR15 38 C1
Longmoor Cl B97 34 C3
Longmynd Way DY13 37 A7
Longridge Rd WR14 27 E4
Lorne Gro DY10 31 G5
Lorne St, Kidderminster DY10 31 G5
Lorne St, Stourport-on-Severn DY13 36 D3
Lorne Ter DY10 31 G5
Loughmill Rd WR10 33 B6
Love La B47 29 A2
Loves Gro WR1 41 B1
Low Field La B97 34 C4
Lowans Hill Vw B97 35 E5
Lowe La DY11 30 C1
Lowell St WR1 42 C3
Lower Chase Rd WR14 27 F1
Lower Chestnut St WR1 42 C3
Lower Field Ter WR5 42 C6
Lower Gambolds La B60 17 E8
Lower Howsell Rd WR14 25 E2
Lower Leys WR11 23 E2
Lower Lickhill Rd DY13 36 B3
Lower Meadow WR9 19 C6
Lower Mill St DY10 31 E4
Lower Montpelier Rd WR14 26 A1
Lower Parklands DY11 30 D5
Lower Pk DY12 15 E4
Lower Priest La WR10 33 C7
Lower Quest Hills Rd WR14 24 D3
Lower Rd WR14 24 D4
Lower Shepley La B60 40 F4
Lower Wilton Rd WR14 27 F1
Lower Wyche Rd WR14 26 C4
Lowesmoor WR1 41 D2
Lowesmoor Pl WR1 41 E1
Lowesmoor Ter WR1 41 E1
Lowesmoor Trading Est WR1 41 D2
Lowesmoor Wharf Est WR1 41 D1
Loweswater Rd DY13 36 B1
Lucerne Av WR14 27 E4
Ludgate Av DY11 30 B6
Ludlow Rd B97 35 F6
Lutterworth Cl WR4 43 F3
Lychgate WR1 41 C3
Lydes Rd WR14 27 F1

Lydham Cl B98 35 G3
Lygon Bank WR14 24 D5
Lygon Cl B98 35 H4
Lynbrook Cl B47 29 C1
Lynden Cl B61 16 B3
Lyndholm Rd DY10 31 G4
Lyndhurst Dr DY10 31 F2
Lynwood Wr WR11 22 B3
Lyttleton Av B60 17 C6
Lyttleton Rd, Bewdley DY12 14 D3
Lyttleton Rd, Droitwich Spa WR9 19 D6
Lyttleton Rd WR10 32 D3
Lyttleton St WR1 42 A1
Mabey Av B98 35 G3
Macauley Rise WR14 25 E4
Madford Retail Park WR14 25 G2
Madresfield Rd WR14 25 E6
Main St, Aldington WR11 23 H2
Main St, Offenham WR11 21 F3
Main St, Offenham WR11 21 F4
Main St, Pershore WR10 32 D2
Malcolm Av B61 16 B3
Malfield Av B97 34 B6
Malham Rd DY13 36 C1
Malinshill Rd WR11 22 B3
Mallard Cl B98 35 G4
Mallard Pl WR9 18 F4
Mallory Dr DY11 31 E1
Mallow Cl WR14 27 G2
Mallow Cres DY10 31 F6
Mallow Dr B61 16 D1
Malt House Mews*, Church St WR15 38 B3
Malt House Walk*, Dog La DY12 15 E3
Malton Cl WR14 24 C1
Malus Cl WR14 25 G4
Malvern Cl DY13 37 B7
Malvern Rd, Bromsgrove B61 17 B7
Malvern Rd, Worcester WR2 42 A6
Malvern Technology Centre WR14 27 F2
Manby Rd WR14 27 E1
Mandeville Way B61 16 D1
Manning Rd WR9 19 C5
Manor Av DY11 30 A3
Manor Av South DY11 30 B4
Manor Cl, Droitwich Spa WR9 19 E5
Manor Cl, Kidderminster DY11 30 B4
Manor Cl, Stourport-on-Severn DY13 36 E3
Manor Court Rd B60 17 C6
Manor Gdns WR10 33 D8
Manor Rd, Birmingham B47 29 B6
Manor Rd, Stourport-on-Severn DY13 36 E3
Mansfield Way WR14 25 G4
Mansion Gdns WR11 22 D3
Mapit Pl WR4 43 H2
Maple Av, Pershore WR10 33 C6
Maple Av, Worcester WR4 43 F3
Maple Cl, Evesham WR11 23 F4
Maple Cl, Kidderminster DY11 30 B2
Maple Cl, Stourport-on-Severn DY13 36 B4
Maple Gro WR9 19 D7
Maple Rd WR14 25 G4
Mappleborough Cl B97 34 C4
March Gro DY12 15 E2

Marchwood Cl B97 34 C3
Marchon Cl WR9 19 F7
Mark Cl WR14 24 C1
Market Pas WR1 41 D3
Market Pl B98 35 F5
Market St, Bromsgrove B61 16 D4
Market St, Kidderminster DY10 31 E5
Market St, Tenbury Wells WR15 38 B3
Market Way DY9 28 E1
Marlborough Av B60 17 E6
Marlborough Cotts B60 17 E6
Marlborough Dr DY13 37 C8
Marlborough Gdns WR14 25 E1
Marlbrook Gdn B61 40 D1
Marlbrook La B60 40 F1
Marlowe Cl DY10 31 H4
Marlpool Cl DY11 30 C2
Marlpool Dr B97 35 E6
Marlpool La DY11 30 C1
Marpool Cl DY11 30 D3
Marpool Pl DY10 30 C2
Marsden Rd B98 35 G6
Marsh Av WR4 43 H2
Marsh Cl WR14 25 F5
Marsh Gro DY10 31 E2
Marsh Way B61 40 B2
Mart La DY13 37 D5
Martin Av WR11 22 A4
Martin Cl, Bromsgrove B61 17 B5
Martin Cl, Malvern WR14 25 G6
Martingale Cl B60 17 C8
Martins Way DY13 37 C5
Martley Rd DY13 37 B7
Marymans Rd WR11 22 B4
Mason Cl WR14 25 F4
Mason Rd DY11 30 C4
Masons Ct WR11 23 E2
Masons Ryde WR10 33 C7
Masters Cl WR11 23 E3
Mathias Cl WR14 25 E2
Mathon Rd WR14 24 A6
Matravers Rd WR14 25 F5
Maund Cl B60 17 B7
May Av WR4 43 E3
May Bank WR14 25 F4
May Farm Cl B47 29 B2
May La B47 29 B2
May Tree Hill WR9 19 E7
May Trees B47 29 B3
Mayberry Ct DY13 36 B4
Maycroft WR11 22 D4
Mayfair WR11 22 D4
Mayfield Av WR3 42 D2
Mayfield Cl, Bromsgrove B61 40 B1
Mayfield Cl, Kidderminster DY11 30 B2
Mayfield Ct DY11 30 D3
Mayfield Rd, Malvern WR14 25 G6
Mayfield Rd, Pershore WR10 33 C5
Mayfield Rd, Worcester WR3 42 D1
Mayflower Cl, Malvern WR14 27 F1
Mayflower Cl, Stourport-on-Severn DY13 37 E6
Mayflower Rd WR9 19 F6
Mayhurst Cl B47 29 D2
Mayhurst Rd B47 29 D2
Maypole Cl DY12 15 F3
McConnell Cl B60 17 F7
McNaught Cl WR1 42 C3
Mead Way WR14 24 D2
Meade Ct*, Merstow Pl WR11 22 C2
Meadow Cft, Birmingham B47 29 C6

Meadow Cft, Stourbridge DY9 28 B3
Meadow Cl WR9 18 B3
Meadow Ct WR9 18 B3
Meadow Grn WR9 18 B3
Meadow Hill Cl DY11 30 B5
Meadow La B48 12 D3
Meadow Mill WR15 38 B5
Meadow Orchard WR12 13 B6
Meadow Piece WR9 18 B3
Meadow Pl WR9 18 C3
Meadow Rd, Birmingham B47 29 B6
Meadow Rd, Bromsgrove B61 40 B2
Meadow Rd, Droitwich Spa WR9 18 B4
Meadow Rd, Malvern WR14 25 E4
Meadow Rise, Bewdley DY12 15 F2
Meadow Rise, Tenbury Wells WR15 38 C1
Meadow Sweet Pl DY10 31 E2
Meadow Vw DY13 37 B8
Meadow Walk, Droitwich Spa WR9 18 B3
Meadow Walk, Pershore WR10 33 D5
Meadow Way WR9 18 B3
Meadowhill Cres B98 35 G3
Meadowhill Rd B98 35 G3
Meadows End WR11 22 B3
Meadowsweet Ct WR14 27 G3
Meadowvale Rd B60 40 E4
Mealcheapen St WR1 41 D2
Medici Rd B60 16 F4
Medway Rd, Evesham WR11 23 F3
Medway Rd, Worcester WR5 43 E4
Melbourne Av B61 16 B2
Melbourne Cl B61 16 C3
Melbourne Rd B61 16 B3
Melbourne St WR3 42 C1
Melen St B97 35 F4
Melrose Cl WR2 42 A4
Mendip Cl, Bromsgrove B61 16 D1
Mendip Cl, Malvern WR14 25 F6
Mendip Cl, Worcester WR4 43 F3
Menston Cl WR4 43 G2
Mentieth Cl DY13 36 B1
Mercia Cl B60 17 C7
Mercia Dr WR9 18 A1
Merick Rd WR14 25 F2
Meridan Pl B60 17 E5
Merricks Cl DY12 14 C3
Merricks La DY12 14 C3
Merrievale Ct WR14 27 F2
Merrill Gdns B60 40 F1
Merrimans Ct WR3 42 C2
Merrimans Hill Rd WR3 42 C2
Merrimans Walk WR3 42 C2
Merry La WR11 21 H4
Merrybrook WR11 22 A3
Mersey Rd WR5 43 E4
Merstow Grn WR11 22 C2
Merstow Pl WR11 22 C2
Merton Cl, Kidderminster DY10 31 H4
Merton Cl, Worcester WR4 43 E3
Merton Rd WR14 25 E3
Michael Cres WR14 24 D1
Michael Tippett Dr WR4 43 G2
Middle Hollow Dr WR4 43 E4
Middle House Dr B60 40 F1
Middle La B47 29 A5
Middle Rd WR2 42 A6
Middle St WR11 41 D1
Middlefield La DY9 28 C2
Middlefield Rd B60 17 E6
Middlehouse La B98 35 F3

Middles Av WR4 43 H2
Middleton Gdns WR4 43 H1
Middleton Rd, Bromsgrove B61 16 D2
Middleton Rd, Kidderminster DY11 30 D1
Midhurst Cl WR5 43 E6
Midland Rd WR4,5 41 F3
Milestone Dr DY9 28 B3
Milestone Rd WR8 39 A4
Milford Av DY13 36 B2
Mill Av WR12 13 A6
Mill Bank WR11 22 D2
Mill Bank Cotts*, Mill La DY11 30 D3
Mill Cl, Birmingham B47 29 B2
Mill Cl, Bromsgrove B60 17 C7
Mill Cl, Stourport-on-Severn DY13 36 F4
Mill La, Bromsgrove B61 16 D4
Mill La, Kidderminster DY11 30 D4
Mill La, Malvern WR14 27 G3
Mill La, Pershore WR10 33 C5
Mill La, Stourport-on-Severn DY13 36 F4
Mill Lane Cl WR10 33 D5
Mill Rd, Evesham WR11 22 B4
Mill Rd, Stourport-on-Severn DY13 36 E4
Mill St, Evesham WR11 22 D2
Mill St, Kidderminster DY11 30 D4
Mill St, Redditch B97 35 F4
Mill St, Worcester WR5 42 C6
Mill Wood Dr WR4 43 H3
Milldale Cl DY10 31 F2
Millennium Way WR11 23 E6
Miller Cl B60 17 B8
Miller St WR9 19 D5
Millers Cl WR4 43 F1
Millers Ct*, Mill La DY11 30 D3
Millfield Rd B61 17 B5
Millhams Av WR4 43 H1
Millpool Cl DY9 28 B4
Millrace Rd B98 35 G3
Mills Cl WR12 13 C5
Millsbro Rd WR98 35 G5
Millside Ct DY12 15 E3
Milret Cl WR3 42 C2
Milton Cl, Kidderminster DY11 30 A4
Milton Cl, Worcester WR3 42 C1
Milton Dr DY9 28 E1
Milton Rd B61 40 C2
Minge La WR8 39 C3
Minster Ct DY13 36 D4
Minster Rd DY13 36 D4
Minster Walk B61 40 B2
Minter Av WR9 19 D6
Minton Mews*, Carlyle Rd B60 17 E6
Mitre Cl*, The Strand B61 16 D4
Mitton Cl DY13 36 D4
Mitton Gdns DY13 36 D4
Mitton St DY13 37 D5
Mitton Walk DY13 37 D5
Moat Cres WR14 25 G6
Moatway WR14 25 G6
Moffit Way DY13 36 C4
Monks Cl WR10 33 C7
Monks Path B97 34 B5
Monnon Cl WR14 27 H1
Monnow WR9 19 C8
Monsell La WR8 39 A4
Monserrat Rd B60 17 F5
Montfort St WR11 23 F2
Montgomery Cl B61 40 C1
Montpelier Rd WR14 24 A6

52

Name	Ref
Waterloo St DY10	31 F4
Waterside, Droitwich Spa WR9	18 E4
Waterside, Evesham WR11	22 C4
Waterside CI WR9	18 F4
Waterside Grange DY10	31 E2
Waterworks Rd WR1	42 A1
Waterworks Walk WR1	42 A1
Watery La DY13	37 E7
Watkins Way WR14	27 G2
Watt CI B61	17 C5
Watt Ct DY13	36 D3
Waveney Rd WR9	19 B7
Waverley CI DY10	31 G2
Weaver CI WR9	19 F5
Weavers Wharf DY10	31 E5
Wedderburn Rd WR14	27 G1
Wedgebourne CI WR9	19 D6
Weethley Ho*, Lock CI B49	34 C5
Weights La B97	34 D1
Weir Gdns WR10	33 D7
Welbeck Dr WR9	30 C5
Welch Gate DY12	14 D3
Welcome Dr B61	40 C1
Well La B60	16 E4
Welland CI WR9	19 B7
Welland Rd WR8	39 A4
Wellesbourne CI B98	35 G4
Wellington CI WR1	41 E3
Wellington Rd B60	17 E6
Wellington St B98	35 F5
Wells CI DY11	30 A4
Wells Gdns WR12	13 C5
Wells Rd, Malvern WR14	26 C2
Wells Rd, Worcester WR5	43 G4
Wendron CI B60	16 E4
Wenlock Dr B61	16 D2
Wenlock Way DY13	37 B7
Wensleydale WR9	19 B6
Werstan CI WR14	27 F2
Wesley Av DY13	37 C7
Wesley Walk B60	17 B7
West Av B98	35 F6
West Malvern Rd WR14	24 A6
West Park Dr WR9	18 B4
West Rd B60	16 E4
West St, Droitwich Spa WR9	19 C5
West St, Evesham WR11	22 C2
West St, Redditch B98	35 F6
Westbourne CI, Bromsgrove B61	17 C5
Westbourne CI, Worcester WR2	42 A4
Westbourne St DY12	15 F3
Westbourne Ter*, Worcester Rd B61	17 C5
Westbury Av WR9	19 A6
Westbury St WR1	41 E1
Westcroft St*, Ombersley St WR9	19 D6
Western Hill CI B96	13 B1
Western Rd DY9	28 C3
Western Way DY11	30 B5
Westfields B61	40 A2
Westlands Walk WR9	18 B3
Westlyn CI WR14	25 E4
Westmead CI WR9	19 C5
Westminster Bank WR14	24 A6
Westminster CI B61	17 B5
Westminster Rd, Kidderminster DY11	30 A4
Westminster Rd, Malvern WR14	26 C5
Westminster Rd, Worcester WR5	43 G5
Westville Av DY11	30 B5
Westward Rd WR14	24 C1
Westwood Av WR9	19 D6
Westwood CI WR9	19 A5
Westwood Rd WR9	18 B4
Westwood Way WR9	19 A5
Wey CI WR9	19 B6
Wey PI WR9	19 B6
Wharfdale Dr WR4	43 G2
Wharfedale Cres WR9	19 A7
Wharfside WR9	18 B1
Wheatcroft Av DY12	15 F2
Wheatridge Rd B60	17 A7
Wheeler CI WR2	42 A4
Wheeler Orchard WR15	38 B5
Wheelers La B97	34 D3
Wheelwright CI, Bromsgrove B60	17 B7
Wheelwright CI, Worcester WR4	43 F1
Whitborn CI WR14	27 G1
Whitborn End WR14	27 G1
Whitburn CI DY11	30 C5
Whitcroft Rd WR10	33 C6
White Heart CI DY12	14 C3
White Hill WR4	43 G1
White House La WR15	38 D4
White Ladies CI WR1	42 B2
White Ladies Walk*, White Ladies CI WR1	42 B2
Whitehouse Rd WR1	42 B2
Whitethorn Gro WR14	25 G4
Whitford CI WR1	17 B6
Whitford Rd B61	16 A4
Whittaker CI WR10	33 B6
Whittles Ct DY11	30 C2
Whitville CI DY11	30 D3
Wick House CI WR14	33 E8
Wickhamford La WR11	23 G4
Wilden La DY13	36 F4
Wildmoor La B61	40 B2
Wildwood Dr WR5	43 H6
Wilfred CI WR3	42 C2
Willets Rd WR9	19 D8
William Bullock CI DY13	37 C5
William Coley PI DY13	37 D7
William Cres WR11	22 C2
William Shakespeare PI WR9	19 D8
William Tennant Way WR8	39 D4
Williamson Rd WR5	43 E4
Willis St DY11	30 C5
Willow Bank WR10	32 F4
Willow Brook Rd B48	12 C2
Willow CI, Bromsgrove B61	16 C4
Willow CI, Pershore WR10	33 A6
Willow CI, Pinvin WR10	32 E1
Willow CI, Stourbridge DY9	28 B3
Willow CI, Worcester WR8	39 F2
Willow Ct, Droitwich Spa WR9	18 B4
Willow Ct, Worcester WR1	42 C6
Willow Dr WR9	19 D7
Willow Gdns B61	16 C3
Willow Gro WR14	25 E4
Willow Rd, Bromsgrove B61	16 B3
Willow Rd, Evesham WR11	23 F4
Willow Way B97	34 D5
Willowdene DY13	37 F5
Willowfield Dr DY11	30 D2
Wilmcote Ct B61	17 B6
Wilmcote Ho*, Cardy CI B97	34 C5
Wilmore La B47	29 A6
Wilmot Rd WR14	24 D2
Wilson St WR1	42 D3
Wilton Av DY11	30 B3
Wilton Rd WR14	27 F1
Winbrook DY12	14 D3
Winchester Av DY11	30 A4
Winchester CI DY9	28 C1
Windermere Dr WR4	43 G1
Windermere Way DY13	36 B2
Windles Row WR4	43 H2
Windmeres WR11	23 E4
Windmill CI DY13	37 C7
Windrush CI DY11	30 C5
Windrush Cres WR14	27 H1
Windrush Rd B47	29 C2
Winds Point DY9	28 C1
Windsor CI WR14	25 G1
Windsor Dr, Kidderminster DY10	31 E3
Windsor Dr, Stourport-on-Severn DY13	37 C8
Windsor Gdns B60	16 D4
Windsor Rd, Droitwich Spa WR9	19 D7
Windsor Rd, Evesham WR11	22 D1
Windsor Rd, Redditch B97	35 E4
Windsor Row WR1	41 D2
Windsor St, Bromsgrove B60	16 D4
Windsor St, Redditch B97	35 F5
Winnetts La WR9	19 D5
Winslow Av WR9	19 F5
Winstone CI B98	35 H5
Winterfold CI DY10	31 H4
Wintour Walk B60	17 B7
Winyate Hill B98	35 H6
Wiselack PI WR4	43 H3
Withers Rd WR2	42 A6
Within Cft WR4	43 H3
Withybed CI B48	12 C3
Withybed Green*, Withybed La B48	12 B4
Withybed La B48	12 B4
Witley Way DY13	37 B8
Witton Av WR9	19 B7
Woburn St B61	17 B5
Wolsey CI WR4	43 E3
Wolverhampton Rd DY10	31 G1
Wolverley Rd DY11	30 C1
Wolverton Rd WR1	42 C3
Wood Av DY11	30 C3
Wood Cft B47	29 D3
Wood Leason Av WR4	43 H2
Wood St DY11	30 D4
Wood Ter, Pershore WR10	33 B8
Wood Ter, Worcester WR1	42 C3
Woodbank Dr B61	40 B2
Woodbine Rd WR1	42 B2
Woodbury Rd DY13	36 C3
Woodbury Rd North DY13	36 C3
Woodbury Rd West DY13	36 C3
Woodbury Rise WR14	24 C3
Woodchester DY9	28 D3
Woodfield B98	35 H4
Woodfield Cres DY13	30 D5
Woodfield Rd WR9	18 E4
Woodfield St DY11	30 D4
Woodfields WR9	18 F4
Woodgate Ho*, Cardy CI B97	34 C5
Woodgreen Dr WR4	43 H3
Woodhampton CI DY13	37 C8
Woodhill CI WR4	43 H2
Woodland Av, Kidderminster DY11	30 C3
Woodland Av, Stourbridge DY8	28 B2
Woodland Piece WR11	23 E5
Woodland Rd B97	34 C5
Woodlands WR11	23 E5
Woodleaves B47	29 B1
Woodman La DY9	28 F3
Woodmans CI WR9	18 B3
Woodmans Grn WR9	18 B4
Woodmans PI WR9	18 B3
Woodmans Rise WR9	18 B3
Woodmans Way WR9	18 B3
Woodrow CI B61	40 B1
Woodrow La B61	40 C2
Woodrush Dr B47	29 C4
Woodshears Dr WR14	27 E2
Woodshears Rd WR14	26 D2
Woodside Rd WR5	43 E6
Woodthorpe Dr DY12	14 D2
Woodward CI WR10	33 B8
Woodward Rd WR10	33 B8
Woolhope Rd WR4	42 C6
Wooton CI B97	34 B4
Worcester CI DY9	28 C3
Worcester Cross Ringway DY10	31 F4
Worcester La DY9	28 D1
Worcester Rd, Bromsgrove B61	17 A8
Worcester Rd, Droitwich Spa WR9	19 D5
Worcester Rd, Evesham WR11	20 A4
Worcester Rd, Malvern WR14	24 D4
Worcester Rd, Pershore WR10	33 A6
Worcester Rd, Stourbridge DY9	28 B4
Worcester Rd, Stourport-on-Severn DY13	37 E5
Worcester Rd, Tenbury Wells WR15	38 B2
Worcester Rd, Wyre Piddle WR10	32 F4
Worcester Rd DY11	31 E6
Worcester St DY10	31 E4
Wordsworth Cres DY10	31 H4
Wordsworth Grn WR14	24 D5
Workman Rd WR11	22 B3
Worth Cres DY13	36 B3
Worthington Gdns WR4	43 H3
Wrekin CI B61	16 D2
Wrekin Walk DY13	37 B7
Wren Av WR14	25 G5
Wych Elm CI WR5	43 E6
Wych Rd WR9	19 C6
Wychavon Way WR9	18 C1
Wychbury Dr DY9	28 E1
Wyche Rd WR14	26 C3
Wye CI, Droitwich Spa WR9	19 C8
Wye CI, Worcester WR5	43 E4
Wykewane WR14	27 G2
Wylds La WR5	41 D4
Wynn CI DY12	15 G1
Wyre Hill, Bewdley DY12	14 C4
Wyre Hill, Pershore WR10	32 E3
Wyre Rd WR10	32 D4
Wythall Green Way B47	29 A6
Wythwood Gro B47	29 D3
Wythwood Rd B47	29 D3
Yarn CI B47	29 B4
Yarranton CI DY13	37 B7
Yates Hay Rd WR14	24 C2
Yeomans Walk B60	17 C6
Yew Tree CI, Bewdley DY12	14 C3
Yew Tree CI, Evesham WR11	23 F5
Yew Tree CI, Redditch B97	34 C5
Yew Tree Ct WR12	13 C6
Yew Tree La DY12	14 C3
Yew Tree Rd DY10	31 G5
Yew Tree Walk DY13	36 B4
Yewleigh La WR8	39 A4
Yewtree Dr B60	16 E4
Yewtree Hill WR9	19 E8
Yock La WR10	33 E6
York Av, Bromsgrove B61	16 C2
York Av, Droitwich Spa WR9	19 D7
York CI, Bromsgrove B61	16 C3
York CI, Malvern WR14	25 F1
York PI, Kidderminster DY10	31 E3
York PI, Worcester WR1	42 B2
York Place La WR1	42 B2
York Rd, Bewdley DY12	14 C3
York Rd, Bromsgrove B61	16 C3
York St, Kidderminster DY10	31 E3
York St, Stourport-on-Severn DY13	37 D5
Zetland Rd WR14	24 D5

www.ESTATE-PUBLICATIONS.co.uk

Red Books - showing the way

For the latest publication list, prices and to order online please visit our website.

LOCAL and SUPER RED BOOKS
(Super Red Books are shown in **Bold** Type)
Abingdon & Didcot
Aldershot & Camberley
Alfreton & Belper
Andover
Ashford & Tenterden
Aylesbury & Tring
Bangor & Caernarfon
Barnstaple & Bideford
Basildon & Billericay
Basingstoke & Andover
Bath & Bradford-upon-Avon
Bedford
Bodmin & Wadebridge
Bournemouth
Bracknell & Wokingham
Brentwood
Brighton
Bristol
Bromley (London Borough)
Burton-upon-Trent & Swadlincote
Bury St. Edmunds & Stowmarket
Cambridge
Cannock & Rugeley
Cardiff
Cardiff City & Bay Visitors Map (Sheet Map)
Carlisle & Penrith
Chelmsford
Chester
Chesterfield & Dronfield
Chichester & Bognor Regis
Chippenham & Calne
Coatbridge & Airdrie
Colchester & Clacton-on-Sea
Corby & Kettering
Coventry
Crawley & Mid Sussex
Crewe
Derby
Dundee & St. Andrews
Eastbourne
Edinburgh
Exeter & Exmouth
Falkirk & Grangemouth
Fareham & Gosport
Flintshire Towns
Folkestone & Dover
Glasgow
Gloucester & Cheltenham
Gravesend & Dartford
Grays & Thurrock
Great Yarmouth & Lowestoft
Grimsby & Cleethorpes
Guildford & Woking
Hamilton & Motherwell
Harlow & Bishops Stortford
Harrogate & Knaresborough
Hastings & Bexhill
Hereford
Hertford & Waltham Cross
High Wycombe
Huntingdon & St. Neots
Ipswich
Isle of Man
Isle of Wight (Complete Coverage)
Kendal & Windermere
Kidderminster
Kingston upon Hull
Lancaster & Morecambe
Leicester
Lincoln
Llandudno & Colwyn Bay
Loughborough & Coalville
Luton & Dunstable
Macclesfield & Wilmslow
Maidstone
Mansfield
Medway & Gillingham
Milton Keynes
New Forest Towns
Newbury & Thatcham
Newport & Chepstow
Newquay & Perranporth
Newtown & Welshpool
Northampton
Northwich & Winsford
Norwich
Nottingham

Nuneaton & Bedworth
Oxford & Kidlington
Penzance & St. Ives
Perth
Peterborough
Plymouth
Portsmouth
Reading & Henley-on-Thames
Redditch & Bromsgrove
Reigate & Mole Valley
Rhyl & Prestatyn
Rugby
St. Albans, Welwyn & Hatfield
St. Austell & Lostwithiel
Salisbury & Wilton
Scarborough & Whitby
Scunthorpe
Sevenoaks
Shrewsbury
Sittingbourne & Faversham
Slough, Maidenhead & Windsor
Solihull
Southampton
Southend-on-Sea
Stafford
Stevenage & Letchworth
Stirling & Alloa
Stoke-on-Trent
Stroud & Nailsworth
Swansea
Swindon
Tamworth & Lichfield
Taunton & Bridgwater
Telford & Newport
Tenby & Saundersfoot (Colour)
Thanet & Canterbury
Torbay
Trowbridge & Frome
Truro & Falmouth
Tunbridge Wells & Tonbridge
Walsall
Warwick & Royal Leamington Spa
Watford & Hemel Hempstead
Wellingborough & Rushden
Wells & Glastonbury
West Midlands & Birmingham (Spiral)
Weston-super-Mare
Weymouth & Dorchester
Winchester
Wolverhampton (Sheet Map)
Worcester
Workington & Whitehaven
Worthing & Littlehampton
Wrexham
York

COUNTY RED BOOKS
(Town Centre Maps)
Bedfordshire
Berkshire
Buckinghamshire
Cambridgeshire
Cheshire
Cornwall
Cumbria
Derbyshire
Devon
Dorset
Essex
Gloucestershire
Hampshire
Herefordshire
Hertfordshire
Kent
Leicestershire & Rutland
Lincolnshire
Norfolk
Northamptonshire
Nottinghamshire
Oxfordshire
Shropshire
Somerset
Staffordshire
Suffolk
Surrey
Sussex (East)
Sussex (West)
Warwickshire
Wiltshire

Worcestershire

EUROPEAN STREET MAPS
Calais & Boulogne Shoppers Map (Sheet Map)
Dieppe Shoppers Map (Sheet Map)
North French Towns Street Atlas

OFFICIAL TOURIST MAPS and TOURIST MAPS
(Official Tourist Maps are shown in **Bold** Type)
-    Kent to Cornwall 1:460,000
1   **South East England** 1:200,000
101 **Kent & East Sussex** 1:150,000
102 **Surrey & Sussex Downs** 1:150,000
103 South East England Leisure Map 1:200,000
104 **Sussex** 1:150,000
2   **Southern England** 1:200,000
201 Isle of Wight 1:50,000
3   **Wessex** 1:200,000
301 Dorset 1:150,000
4   **Devon & Cornwall** 1:200,000
401 **Cornwall** 1:180,000
402 **Devon** 1:200,000
403 **Dartmoor & South Devon Coast** 1:100,000
404 **Exmoor & North Devon** 1:100,000
5   Greater London (M25 Map) 1:80,000
6   **East Anglia** 1:200,000
7   **Chilterns & Thames Valley** 1:200,000
8   **Cotswolds & Severn Valley** 1:200,000
802 The Cotswolds 1:110,000
9   Wales 1:250,000
10 **The Shires of Middle England** 1:250,000
11 **The Mid Shires** (Staffs, Shrops, etc.) 1:200,000
111 **Peak District** 1:100,000
12 Snowdonia 1:125,000
13 **Yorkshire** 1:200,000
131 **Yorkshire Dales** 1:125,000
132 **North Yorkshire Moors** 1:125,000
14 **North West England** 1:200,000
141 **Isle of Man** 1:60,000
15 **North Pennines & Lakes** 1:200,000
151 Lake District 1:75,000
16 **Borders of Scotland & England** 1:200,000
17 **Burns Country** 1:200,000
18 Heart of Scotland 1:200,000
181 **Greater Glasgow** 1:200,000
182 **Edinburgh & The Lothians** 1:150,000
183 **Isle of Arran** 1:63,360
184 **Fife (Kingdom of)** 1:100,000
19 **Loch Lomond** 1:150,000
191 **Argyll, The Isles & Loch Lomond** 1:275,000
20 **Perthshire** 1:150,000
21 **Fort William, Ben Nevis, Glen Coe** 1:185,000
211 Iona and Mull 1:10,000 / 1:115,000
22 **Grampian Highlands** 1:185,000
23 **Loch Ness & Aviemore** 1:150,000
24 **Skye & Lochalsh** 1:130,000
25 **Argyll & The Isles** 1:200,000
26 **Caithness & Sutherland** 1:185,000
27 **Western Isles** 1:125,000
28 **Orkney & Shetland** 1:128,000 } same map
28 **Shetland & Orkney** 1:128,000 }
30 **Highlands of Scotland** 1:275,000
92 **England & Wales** 1:650,000
93 Scotland 1:500,000
94 Historic Scotland 1:500,000
95 Scotland (Homelands of the Clans)
99 Great Britain 1:1,100,000
99 Great Britain (Flat) 1:1,100,000
100 British Isles 1:1,100,000

EUROPEAN LEISURE MAPS
Europe 1:3,100,000
Cross Channel Visitors' Map 1:530,000
France 1:1,000,000
Germany 1:1,000,000
Ireland 1:625,000
Italy 1:1,000,000
Netherlands, Belgium & Luxembourg 1:600,000
Spain & Portugal 1:1,000,000

WORLD MAPS
World Map - Political (Folded) 1:29,000,000
World Map - Political (Flat in Tube) 1:29,000,000
World Travel Adventure Map (Folded) 1:29,000,000
World Travel Adventure Map (Flat in Tube) 1:29,000,000

ESTATE PUBLICATIONS, Bridewell House, Tenterden, Kent. TN30 6EP
Tel: 01580 764225   Fax: 01580 763720   Email: sales@estate-publications.co.uk